I0902388

VOICES OF AMERICA

ROCK HILL
SOUTH CAROLINA
Gateway to the New South

About the Authors

A Winthrop history professor and a former president of the South Carolina Historical Association, Dr. Edward Lee is the author of the award winning *Yorkville To York.* A speech pathologist and accomplished cook, Dr. Anne Beard teaches speech at Winthrop University.

VOICES OF AMERICA

ROCK HILL
SOUTH CAROLINA
Gateway to the New South

Compiled by
J. Edward Lee, Ph.D., and Anne E. Beard, Ed.D.

ARCADIA
PUBLISHING

ISBN 978-0-7385-0350-9

Published by Arcadia Publishing
Charleston, South Carolina

Printed in the United States of America

Library of Congress Catalog Card Number applied for.

For all general information contact Arcadia Publishing at:
Telephone 843-853-2070
Fax 843-853-0044
E-Mail sales@arcadiapublishing.com
For customer service and orders:
Toll-Free 1-888-313-2665

Visit us on the Internet at www.arcadiapublishing.com

Dedication

To Ola and Tyre Lee
Jackie and Ben Frank Hardy;
In Memory of Norman Fohl;
For the Winthrop Family.

Credits: Jason Brown, Ann Evans, Becky Bryant Faris, Carol Hanlon, Ann Lee, Elizabeth Lee, Jackie Lukich, Joel Nichols, Rachel Smith, Catawba Indian Nation, City of Rock Hill, and Winthrop University Archives

Contents

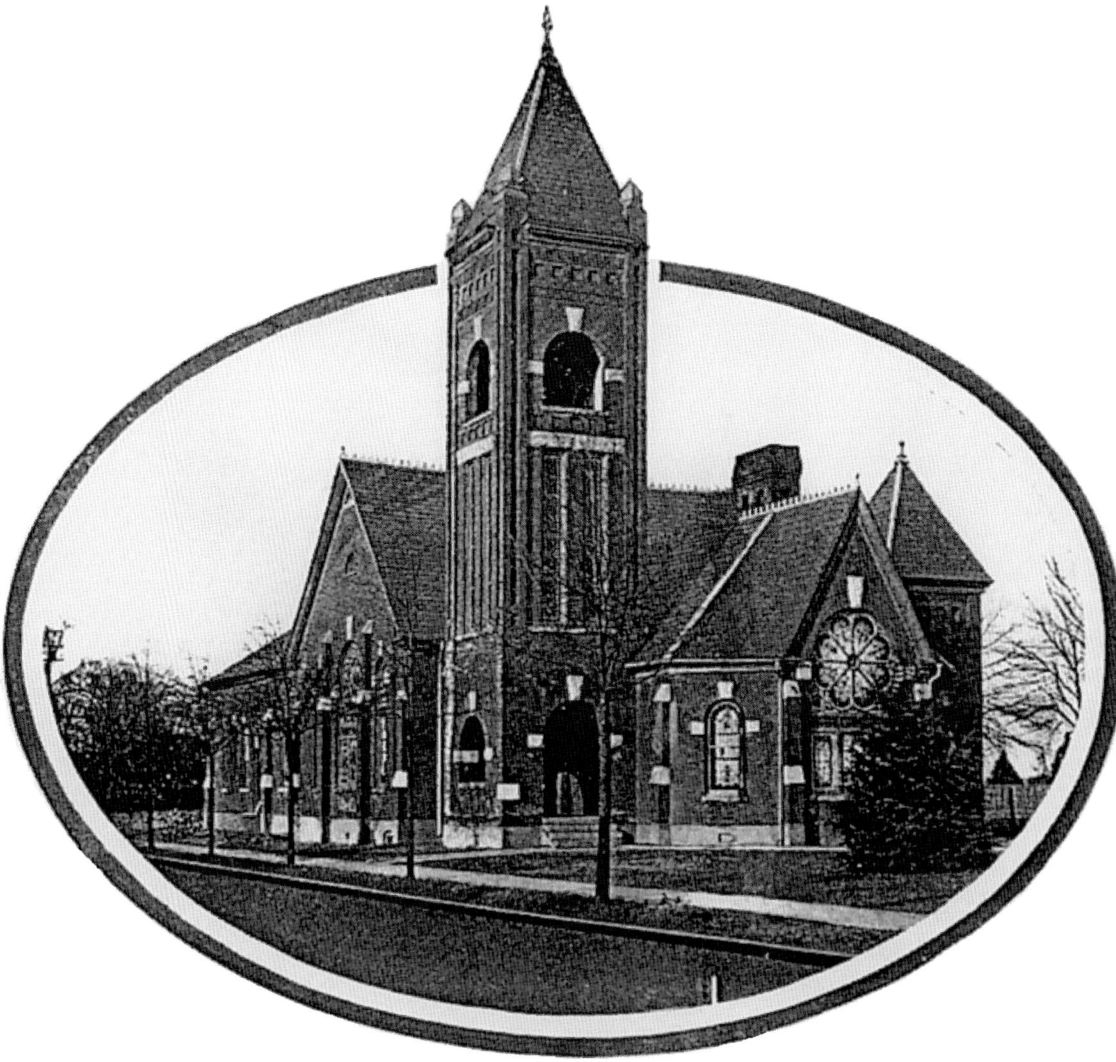

Shown here is the Associate Reformed Presbyterian Church.

INTRODUCTION

"We believe it is to be called Rock Hill"
—Squire John Roddey, 1851

The tranquility of the day after Thanksgiving, 1926, was shattered as a tornado whirled through downtown Rock Hill, South Carolina. The ferocious wind ripped the roof off Dr. David Lyle's hospital on Marion Street. It systematically knocked down all the chimneys on one side of the street and spun a porch swing at the Otis Patton home, ripping it from its hinges and depositing the swing atop a Chinaberry tree. The autumn storm crossed Hampton Street and took aim at the First Presbyterian Church, toppling the sanctuary's steeple. The Associate Reformed Presbyterian Church lost two large stained-glass windows, numerous small windows, and the top of a beautiful cedar tree. Providentially,

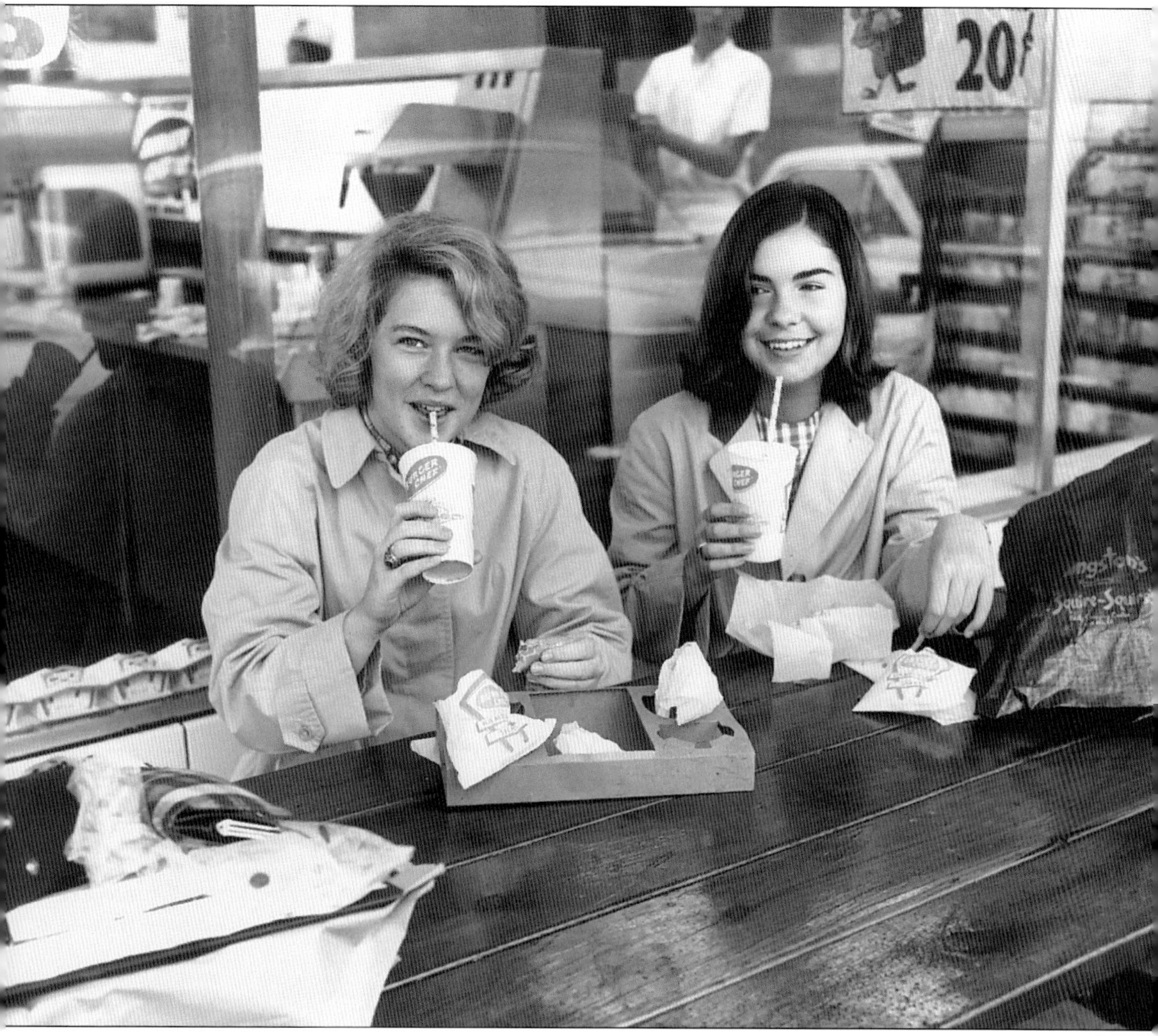

just a month earlier the ARP congregation had wisely purchased a $20,000 tornado insurance policy.

Over 150 businesses and homes were damaged by the 1926 tornado. Several Rock Hillians were injured, and one citizen was killed. At a citywide religious service held shortly after the disaster, the ARP Church's pastor commented, "We can show our thanks to Him for saving the lives of our people...by dedicating our lives to His service in deed, memory and time." And the hard working people of Rock Hill, bruised by a killer storm, joined hands and rebuilt their town.

Rock Hill is a city of survivors and hardy souls who have withstood the destruction of the Civil War, withstood several devastating fires, suffered the calamity of the Great Depression, enlisted in the noble crusade of World War II, witnessed a constantly evolving local economy, and participated in the modern era's social and political tumult. Along the way, for nearly a century and a half, Rock Hillians of all colors and of all ages have built impressive homes, picked cotton beside one another in the fields of Ogden, and worked together in Victoria, Aragon, and J.P. Stevens mills. They have spent leisurely Saturday afternoons at Friedham's Department Store and at the mall, filled the classrooms of institutions

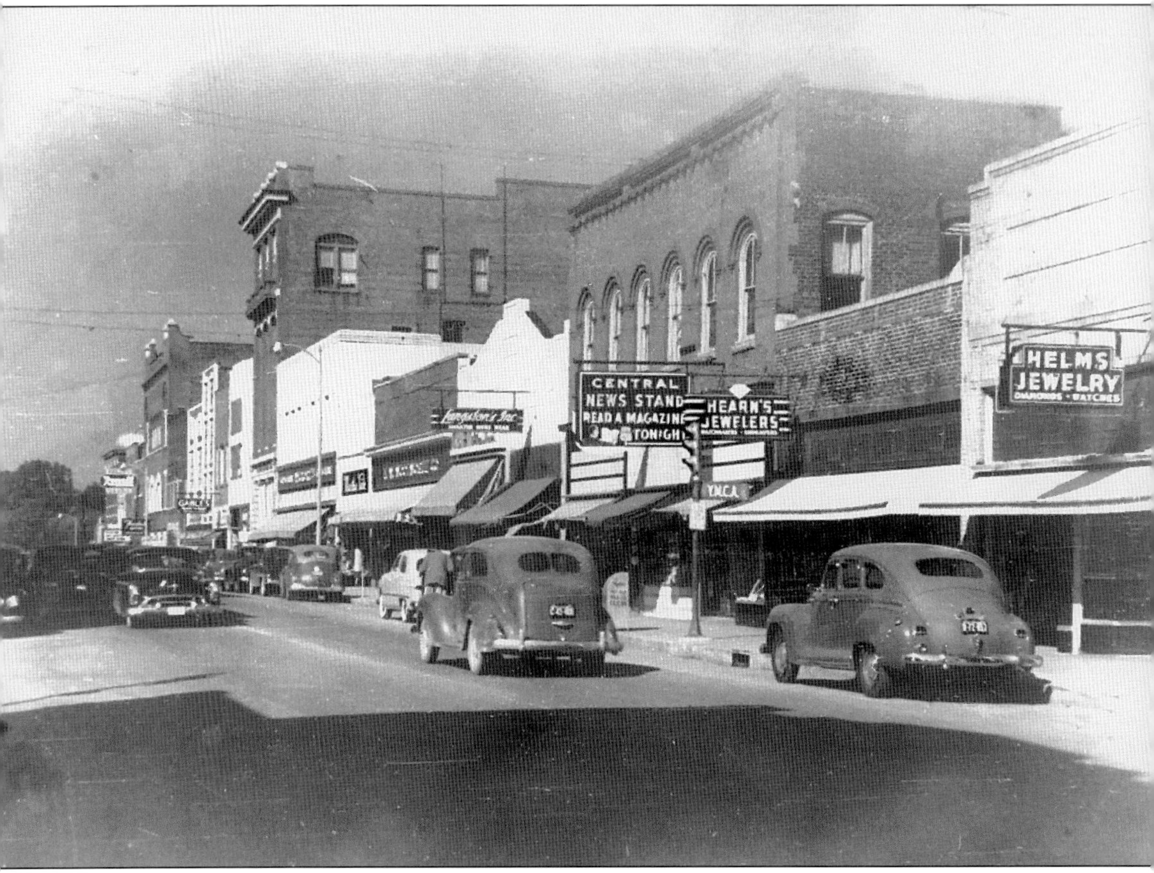

Here is a 1950 view of the east side of Main Street.

named Winthrop, Friendship, and Clinton junior colleges, marketed the inventions of gifted sons and daughters, worshiped in the pews of Boyd Hill and Ebenezer, watered their horses at Crawford Road springs, and celebrated holidays with festive homemade fireballs. They have weathered the flood of 1916, the tornado of 1926, the hurricanes of 1954 and 1989 and countless droughts, addressed past injustices, and shared the good and bad times which flow through the rich history of a town of survivors.

Rock Hill is a "New South" city. As Atlanta newspaperman Henry Grady told a group of New Yorkers in 1886, "There was a South of slavery and secession—that South is dead. There is a South of union and freedom—that South, thank God, is living, breathing, growing every hour." He was speaking about us. Rock Hill is "New South" because, throughout our history, we have been willing to boldly experiment with fresh ideas as we have carved out an identity all our own—not one influenced by Charlotte or those "Old South" towns such as Charleston or Columbia, which have seen so much and lived so long. That is why we have grown from a population of 100 in 1860 to a thriving city of more than 50,000 innovative citizens in the last days of the twentieth century. Our survival after the whirlwind of 1926 is just one example of the unbending spirit of a vibrant "New South" city.

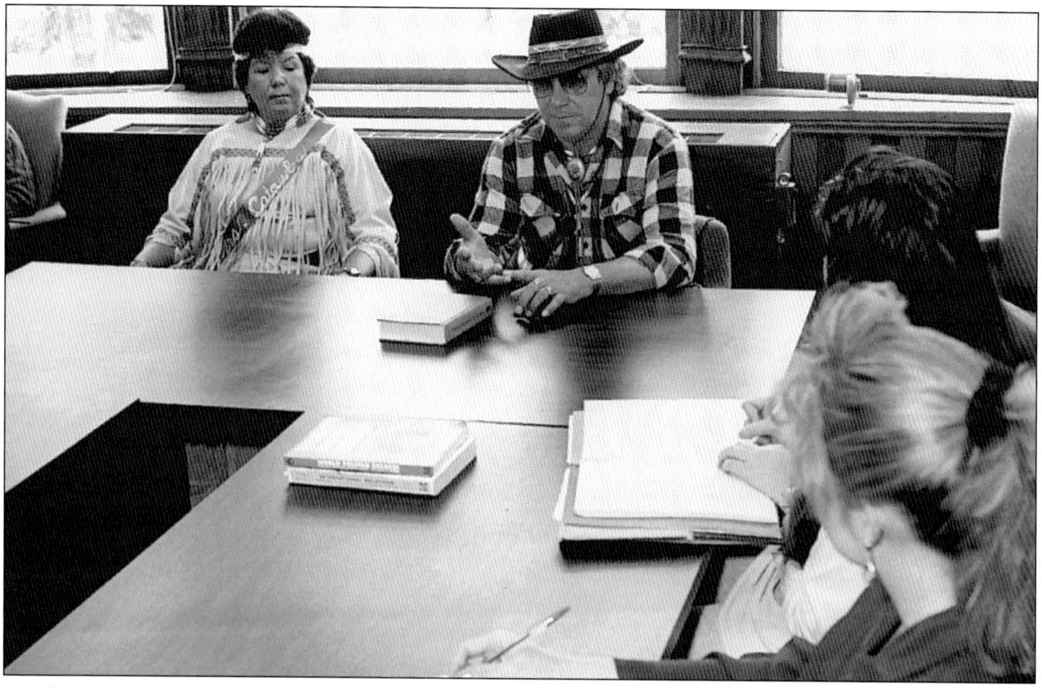

Gail Blue Jones and Catawba Chief Gilbert Blue meet with Winthrop University students in 1992.

SETTLEMENT

No story of this New South city's history can be complete without an acknowledgement of the role played by an ancient people, the Catawba Indian Nation. Thousands of years before Rock Hillians dusted themselves off and reassembled their lives after the 1926 tornado, the Catawbas had filtered down into this area. Hunting and gathering across an enormous slice of the Carolinas, these ancient "people of the river" (ye i swa) laid the foundation for the gateway to the New South.

Once comprising a nation of perhaps 10,000 individuals, the Catawbas made lasting contributions to the region from their trading centers sprinkled throughout the Piedmont. They were in close harmony with nature, and under a rich green canopy, they shared their knowledge of agriculture and hunting with white settlers who made their way onto Catawba land from the Great Wagon Road of the eastern United States.

Unfortunately, these generous "people of the river" endured hardships such as smallpox epidemics, which repeatedly decimated the population, the 1763 murder of their beloved King Hagler at the hands of other American Indians, deaths on Revolutionary and Civil War battlefields, the heartless carving up of their ancestral homeland by encroaching settlers, unsympathetic government officials, and the ugly scars of segregation.

Today, however, the "people of the river" have been resurrected in a typical Rock Hill manner by a comprehensive 1993 settlement with the federal and state governments. Here, Jeff Venables, a Chemistry teacher at Northwestern High School, clearly explains the impact of the 1993 settlement on the tenacious first people of Rock Hill and their neighbors.

"In 1993, an agreement was reached between the Catawba Indian Nation and the governments of the United States and South Carolina. In the deal, the federal government paid $32 million, the state government paid $12.5 million, York and Lancaster Counties combined for $2.6 million, title insurance companies paid $1.4 million, and other private sector sources paid an additional $1.5 million. The total cash settlement was $50,000,000. Other benefits for the Catawbas included federal recognition, ability to expand their reservation, tribal self-government, tax exemptions, and bingo privileges. In exchange, the Catawbas agreed to dismiss all land claims, of which 60,000 to 90,000 existed.

"In the settlement, the Catawba Indian Nation gained federal recognition. This allows the members access to numerous benefits, including special services, educational benefits, medical care, and welfare assistance, as well as grants and loans for housing and reservation development. The benefit that has caused the greatest problem to date is the health care benefits. Health Services, which is a part of the Bureau of Indian Affairs, which falls in the Department of the Interior, provides benefits for approximately 1,500 Catawbas, while there are currently more than 2,000 members trying to use the benefits. The result is that many medical bills have not been paid. The tribe owes many doctors' offices money, forcing a number of doctors to stop accepting patients who have only tribal health insurance. In addition, says Donald Rogers of the Catawba Cultural Preservation Project, the problem has given the Catawbas a 'bad name.' It is hoped that the problem will be remedied when the final tribal roll is finished. Other benefits have proven to be very beneficial for the tribe and its members.

"At the time of the settlement, the reservation was 630 acres. The settlement allows the Catawbas to acquire an additional 3,000 acres under reservation status, including some land that does not need to be contiguous to the existing reservation. After the final tribal roll is completed and published in the Federal Register, the tribe will be allowed to govern itself, holding periodic elections for leadership positions. They may form a tribal council or executive committee to regulate the conduct of members through a tribal court with limited jurisdiction.

"Land on the reservation is exempt from property tax, although vehicles and other property are taxed. There is no state sales tax on the reservation. The members of the tribe do pay income taxes and are assessed payments for children attending public schools in lieu of the school district taxes. This is a point of contention currently, as the school district has filed a suit against the Catawbas for over $200,000 in school payments dating back to 1994. The Catawbas claim that they are not liable for the payments. Donald Rogers stated that a defense of the Catawbas is that no other ethnic group are charged for their children to go to public school. He states, however, that the Catawbas should pay the money if that provision 'is contained in the agreement.' There seems to be some question at this point.

"The federal Indian Gaming Regulatory act does not apply to the Catawba Tribe. This means that the Catawbas do not have the right to operate casinos. The tribe was given the option to sponsor bingo games, with a special license allowing more frequent sessions and higher stakes than allowed other bingo operators in the state. The Catawba Bingo Hall is at the site of the former Rock Hill Mall and showed its first profit in the first quarter of 1999. The tribe has high hopes for bingo and plans on using bingo money for education in the future. Donald Rogers explains that it takes time for any business to start making money, but he and the tribe hope that Catawba Bingo will make over $10 million per year by the year 2010.

"The $50 million settlement was divided into five trust funds. The Catawba Land Acquisition Trust Fund is used to purchase reservation and non-reservation land for the

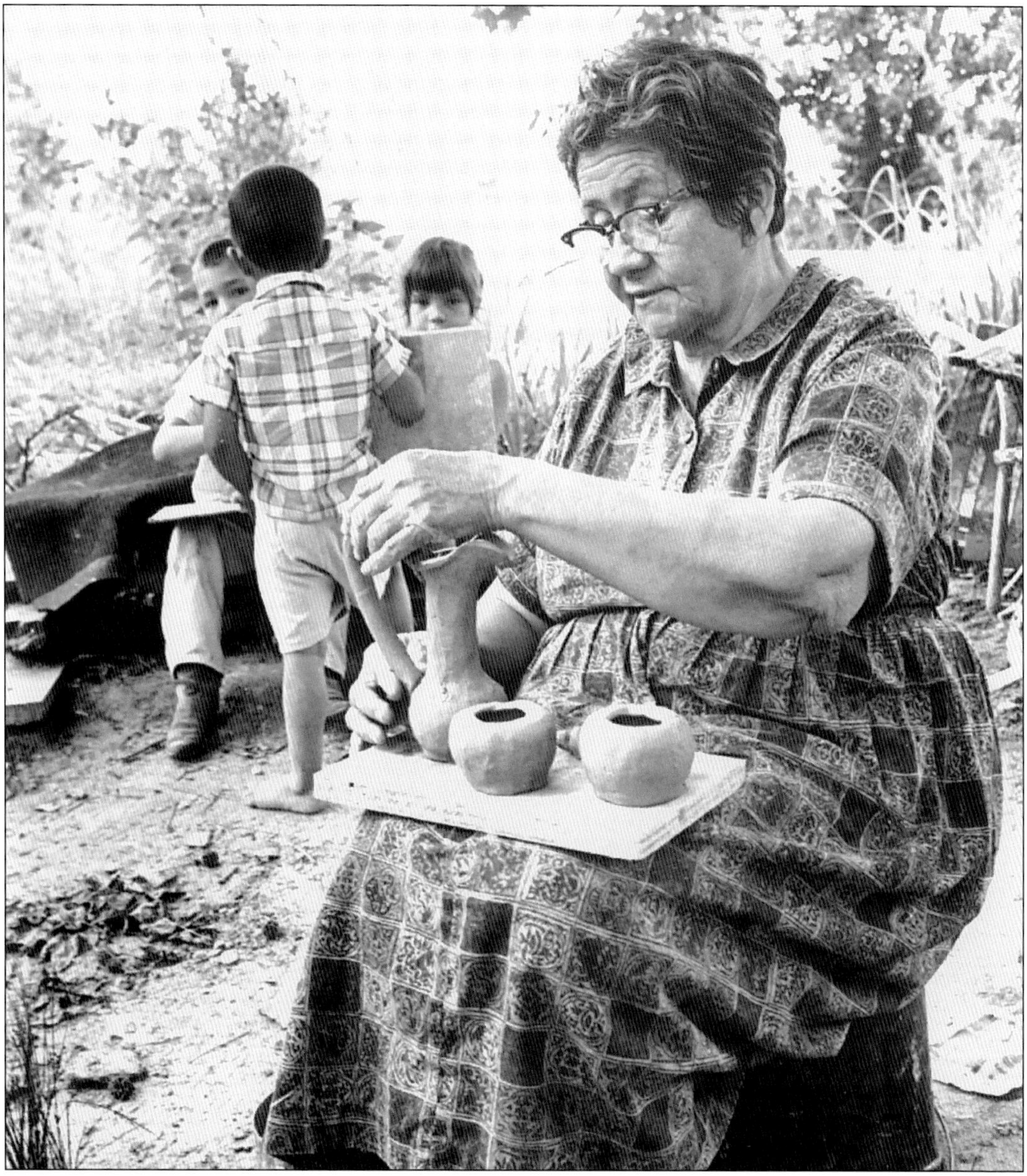

With her grandchildren in the background, this Catawba molds pottery.

nation. This money is used mainly for home sites, but land has also been purchased for the purpose of building a community center to operate as a part of the York County Cultural Heritage Commission, along with the Museum of York County and Brattonsville. Unfortunately, the plans for the center never developed, and the tribe will probably soon sell the land. The Catawba Economic Development Trust Fund is money to be used to develop tribal economic development activities, including tribal business ventures such as bingo. The Catawba Education Trust Fund is mainly used to assist Catawba members with college costs.

"The Catawba Social Services and Elderly Assistance Trust Fund is used for the housing and care of elderly members, as well as the health and welfare of children. This fund also covers substance abuse services. The Catawba Per Capita Payment Trust Fund is established to make a one-time payment to all members whose names appear on the final membership roll. The amount in the fund will be divided by the number of members on the final roll, and each will receive an equal amount from this fund.

"In order to be included on the roll, an individual must be on the membership roll published on February 25, 1961, or 'be a lineal descendant of a member whose name appeared or should have appeared on the membership roll,' according to federal law. The criteria does not include a certain minimum blood quotient, which makes the Catawba settlement different from many others. A minimum Catawba blood quotient of 1/8 was removed from the final agreement. The 'should have appeared' statement has led to an increase in the rolls.

"York County and Rock Hill have benefited significantly from the settlement. An estimated 80,000 landowners were able to breathe easy in the knowledge that their land would not be repossessed by the Catawbas. Economic development has exploded in York County. Before the settlement, individuals and businesses were worried about moving to the area, since they could be in danger of losing their land. Relations between Catawbas and others in York County have improved significantly. The resentment earlier displayed to the Catawbas by York County landowners fearful of losing their land has abated.

"The 1993 settlement has improved life for the Catawba Indians as well. They have used trust funds and HUD grants to build about 60 houses since the settlement. The houses are either sold by the tribe to tribal members at cost or rented to members. The quality of health care has improved, despite the financial problems, and there is a clinic on the reservation to treat members with specific ailments. After the final roll is published, every member of the tribe will receive a payment of about $2500, and the tribe will be able to govern itself. Those who live on the reservation pay no taxes on their homes, there is no sales tax on the reservation or income tax on crafts sold on the reservation, and members that work for the tribe pay no state income taxes. Most importantly, the Catawbas have regained their sense of identity.

"Ask Donald Rogers if the settlement was 'fair' for the Catawbas, and you can guess what the answer would be from someone whose people were removed from 144,000 acres of land. Of course it was not. The livelihood of the Catawba people was taken away. They lost their homes, as well as the land on which they hunted and gathered food. What would be 'fair' would be for the Catawbas to get their land back, along with the 'livelihood' that now exists on it. Since everyone knows that will never happen, the Catawbas have 'settled' for the arrangement I have described. For the most part, the economy and the people of Rock Hill, including the Catawbas, are better off now than they were in 1993, before the settlement was reached."

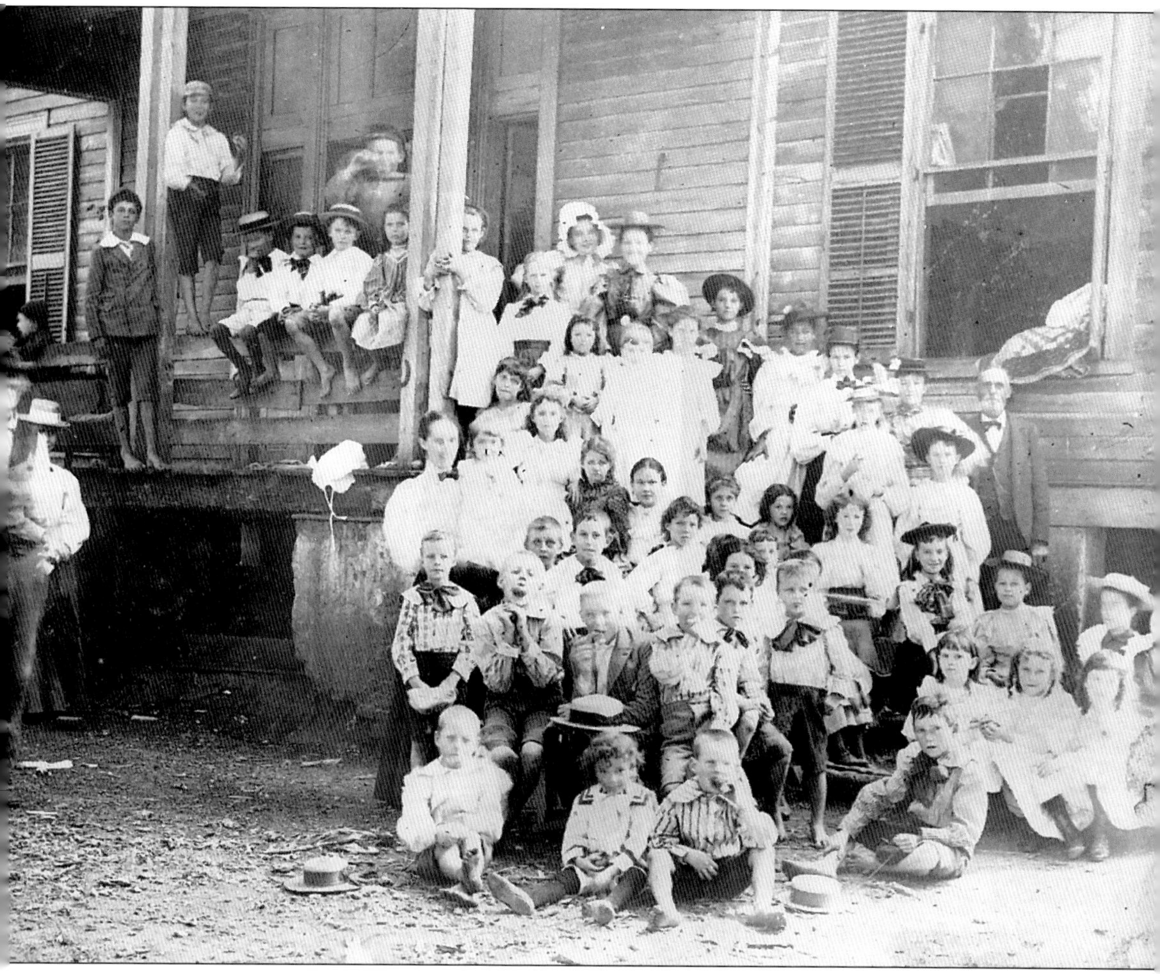

AWAKENING

Blessed with a sparkling memory, Mrs. Sophie Albright hid from the storm of 1926 in a Marion Street basement. The daughter of James Edward Marshall and Fannie Friedham, Mrs. Albright's grandfather, Arnold Friedham, established one of Rock Hill's best-known businesses, Friedham's Department Store, in 1898. At Friedham's, it was agreed, you could purchase anything you needed from farm implements to candy to clothing. Today, Friedham's has evolved into First Union Center, which graces Main Street.

Mrs. Albright recalls a community where no one locked homes or cars, children "had to create [their] own entertainment," wars brought people together, houses rented for $25 a month, substitute teachers earned $5 a day, Phillips Drug Store sold Cokes for 5¢ each, and "it used to be that we knew everyone in Rock Hill." The town was, Mrs. Albright explains, a "friendly, wonderful place to grow up." During a trip to the nation's capital, however, she learned that not all cities were as carefree as Rock Hill; that experience would be her "awakening."

"I remember the first storm that we had that was such a terrible one. It was 1926. A group of girls were around at Mrs. Agnes London, Mrs. John R. London's on Marion Street. We always got together after school and went to one of the friends' houses and made fudge or just talked and had a

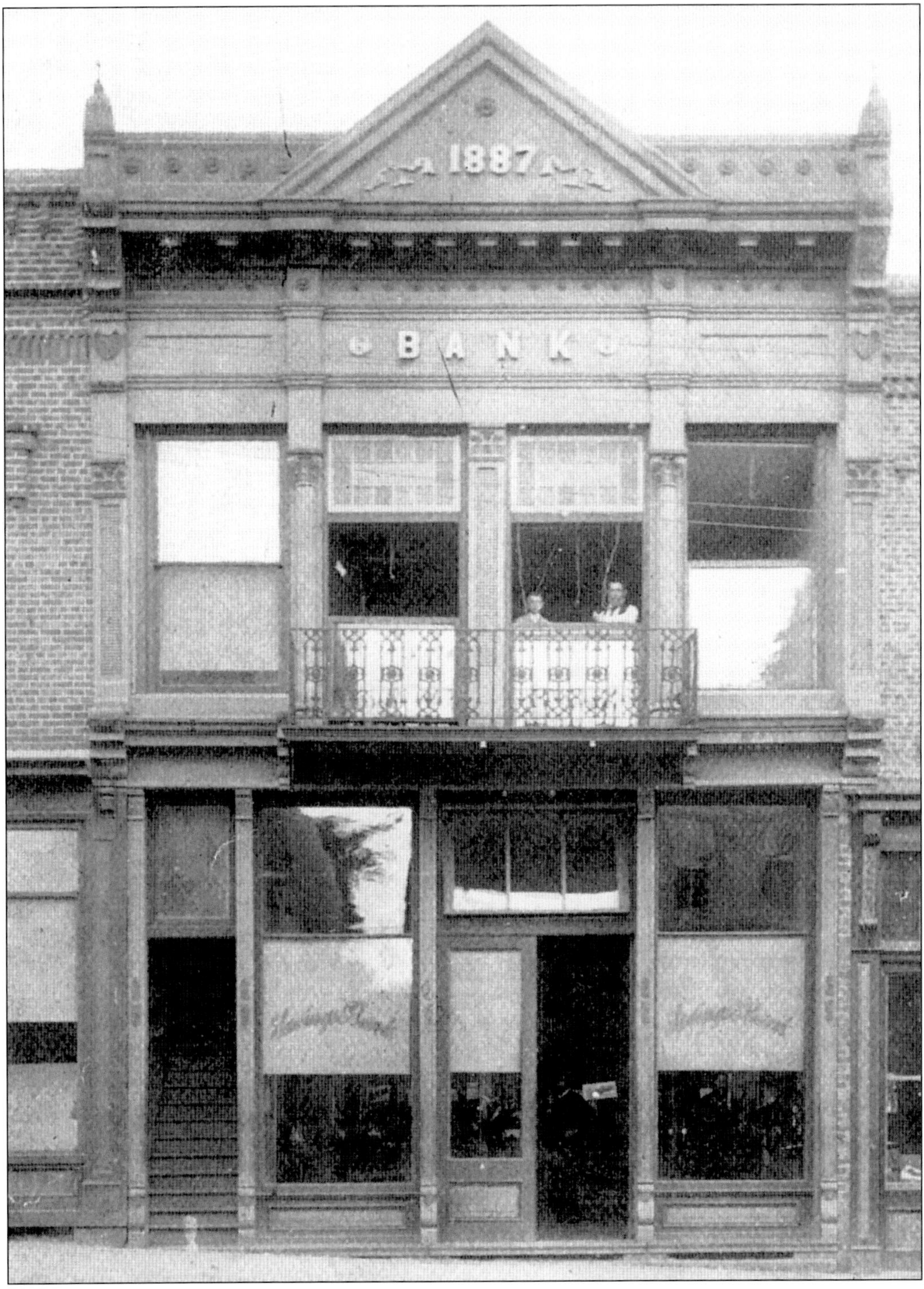

good time, but that particular afternoon this storm came up. It was a cyclone. Miss Agnes herded us all down to the basement, and we stayed down there til the storm was over. When we came out we didn't realize actually what a bad storm it had been, but we looked across the street and Lyle Hospital was practically demolished. There were trees all over the street, and each of us had to walk home because there was no way we could get a ride, so I started down Main Street from Marion Street, and the farther I went, it was obvious that the damage that had been done was terrible. There were trees uprooted, lines across the street. I got to the Presbyterian Church, and the tower was off the church. Then I came on down, and closer home, there was less damage down this way. It didn't hit us. There was a big wedding that night. Margaret McElveen was going to get married at First Presbyterian Church. They went on with the wedding, and it was a beautiful wedding. People just acted as if nothing had happened. The crowd came, and everybody celebrated and had a good time. In the meantime, the Caldwells lived up the street where later the McKnights lived, and Libby was expecting a baby, and I think the baby was not quite due. With all this excitement, the baby arrived, and they called him 'Cyclone Jim.' To this day, I suppose, I don't know where Jim is now, but he was always known as 'Cyclone Jim.'

"It was 1926. There was a lot of damage done on Reid Street, and the old Bright home on White Street was hit to some degree but not that badly. The trees were mostly across the paved streets, paved streets back then. It was a terrifying experience. I was running by the time I got home. I had picked up speed as I got closer home, and by the time I got home, I was out of breath.

"And at Christmas time we shot firecrackers. Of course, we had wonderful Christmas parties. People would have parties and celebrate Christmas. We would hang our stockings and first go to bed and act as if we were surprised after we had snooped around and found out what we were getting. We believed in Santa Claus for a right good little while. And we were so disillusioned when we found out there was no Santa but the spirit of Santa Claus.

"It was really interesting here during World War II. All the men that had been in the service. Well, the original neighborhood was almost in its original being during the war. All the wives, all the people who had grown up in this neighborhood, moved back with their parents, because their husbands were in the service. And we would check on each other daily. We formed a little bridge club and had some good times together, kept each other cheered as well as we could, boosted our spirits, and several of the husbands were in real rough battles during the time. We had a postman who was just a real interesting character. He would come down the street, and he knew most everybody on the street. Naturally, he had been serving this particular area for many years. And he would come down the street, and Laura Morgan was living up the street when Bidie was in the service and he was in a danger area. So the postman would came by and say, 'Well, Laura didn't hear from Bidie again today, and she really is worried about him,' and then he'd come on down and he'd say, 'Well, Lib Kirk heard from Vernon.' He'd come on down and say, 'Well, Mary (Dunlap) didn't hear from Jack again today.' So we'd all kind of get together and then Mary (Hambright) Wise was there, and Joe (Wise) was in the service. There were two neighbors that were not in the service...the Cowans who lived down there. He was 4-F, and he was not able to go, and there was another gentleman down in the next block, Lonnie Abernathy, who was too old to go. So they would try to keep us boosted. Fortunately, my husband, Ickie, never had to go in the danger zone. It was my job to kind of console the rest of them. I felt kind of bad about it. I was happy that I was not in their boat. I felt kind of bad having them go through all that agony, and here I was with a smug little feeling, knowing Ickie was safe. But we did a lot to keep the spirits up.

"It was just great, just absolutely wonderful, when the war ended. But I

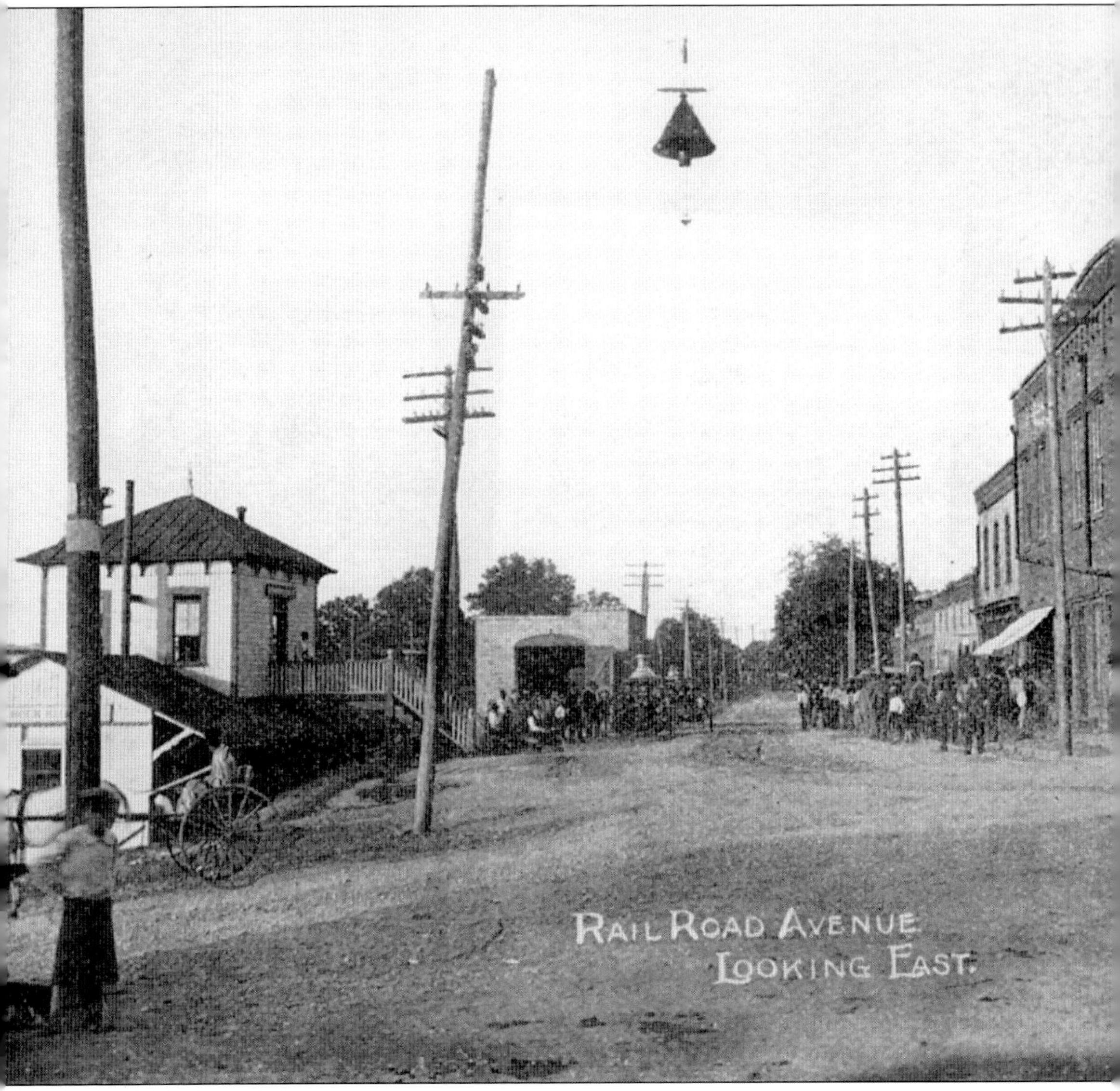

think the memories we had of the war could have been worse, if we hadn't been able to get back with our parents and boosting others was a good thing. But we had to have everything rationed. We toed the line and worked at the Red Cross and knitted sweaters. Then, when we had maneuvers everybody would try to take in the young men. This was before they went overseas. All they wanted, the primary thing the soldiers wanted, and this was before they went into the war, they wanted to get a bath. There was no way they could have a bath. There was a big maneuver down near Steele's Crossing, which is down at the end of Main Street. But those boys would come, back in those days you didn't have a lock on the house because nobody would dare bother you. You didn't lock your cars. You didn't take your keys out of your car. You left the cars parked outside the garage. Usually had it filled with gasoline in case you wanted to take them somewhere, as much as the ration would allow you, anyway. But one Sunday morning, Daddy went out, and his car was gone. He did not get the least bit alarmed; my father was very easy going.

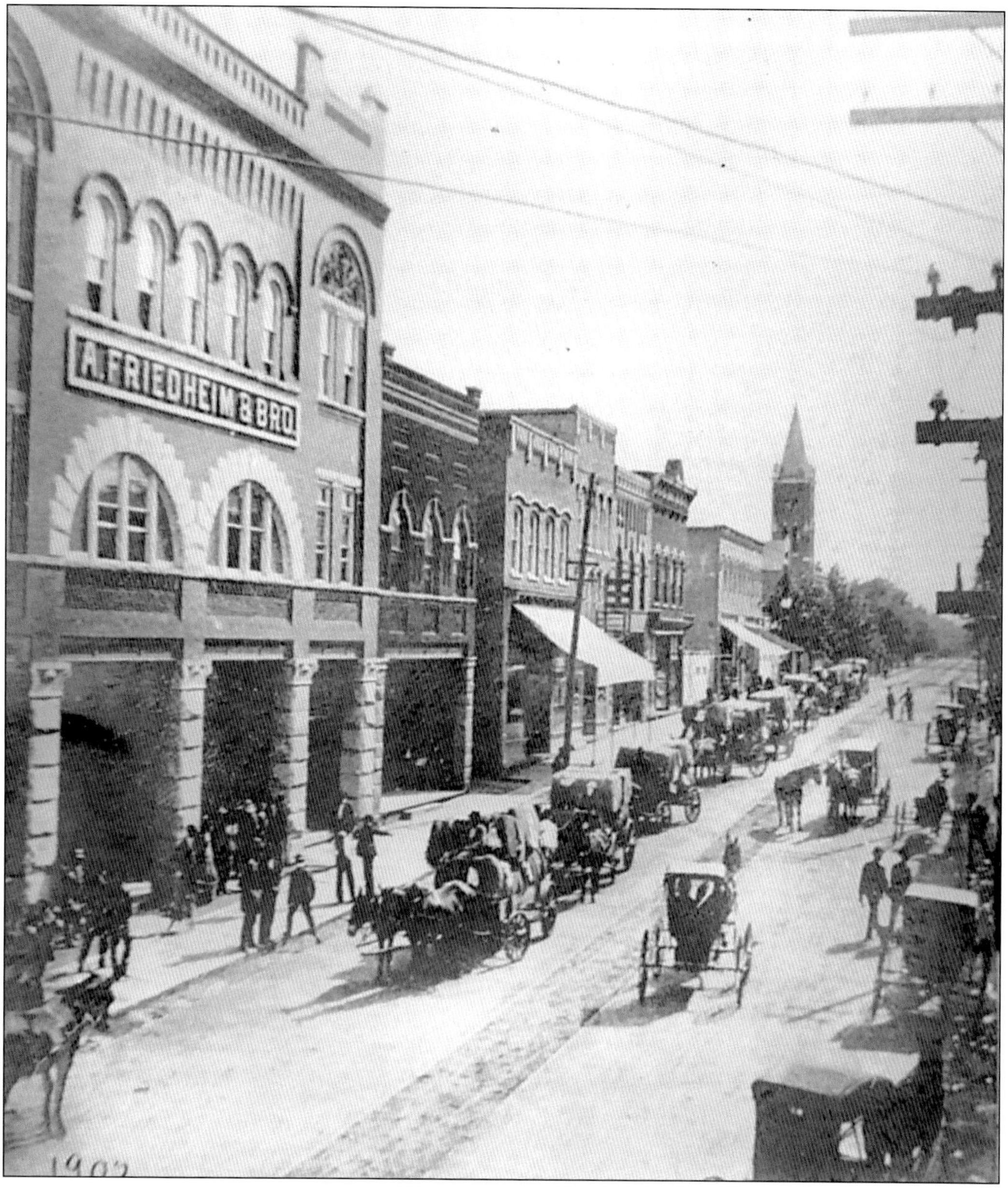

Cotton arrives on Main Street in 1902.

I guess today you'd call him a laid back person; nothing seemed to bother him too much. He took everything in his stride, just saw the good in everybody, and of course Mother was the same way. But Daddy said, 'Well some of the boys just wanted to use my car, and that's alright. I had as much gas in it as I was allowed to put in it. They'll ride in it til they give out of gas, and then I'll just go get my car.' And that was all he did about it. Later, sure enough, the car was found right there in the street, out of gas.

"Sugar and chocolate were rationed during the war. I'm a great chocolate candy lover. Ned, my only child at that time, had been sick. We had to get a doctor's permit to take him down to the beach. We thought

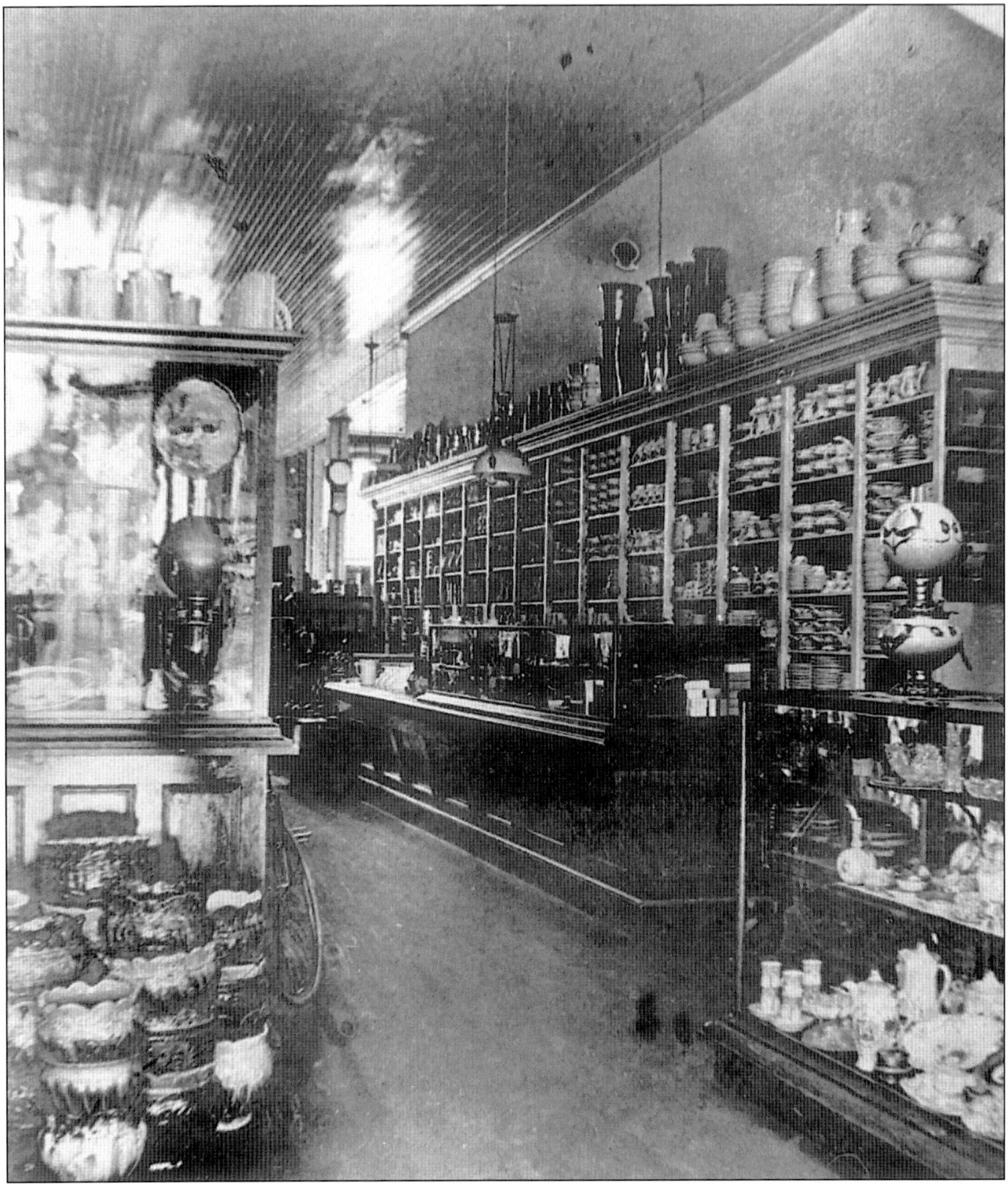

that would do him some good. My brother, Ed, had problems with his back, so he didn't go. He was 4-F, and it upset him so. And he'd say, "I'm not even good enough to serve my country." It was real depressing for those people who could not go. Harriet Marshall and I went down. At the time, she had two children and I only had one. But we went to the beach. We got enough gas to go down, with the doctor's permit. We went to this one little grocery store at Ocean Drive, and by that time, of course, we had the blackouts. We had to have black shades, couldn't go out on the beach after a certain time, and we were actually considered in the danger zone. But we went to this little grocery-drug store and bought our groceries. We went in one time, and the man said, 'I saved you something, one bar of candy, one Hershey Bar.' Oh, we were delighted. We had three children and two adults, and Harriet and I looked at each other cunningly and said, 'Well you know there won't be enough if we get the candy out in front of the children, and they really don't have any business with candy. Let's wait until they go to bed, and we'll eat our candy.' I think that's the most cruel act I ever committed. Harriet and I ate the candy, and I'm sure it must have given us indigestion cause we knew we were doing a sly, wrong thing.

"Ned was in the second grade when Ickie came back from the war. We had lived with Mother and Daddy all during that time. Then we stayed on with them for awhile. Daddy was not well, so we felt they needed somebody with them, so we stayed with them several months, and we had some good renters in our house. We were getting $25 a month for our little house. We thought that was BIG money. We wanted more children, but we didn't get our wish until ten years later. Then Buddy was a welcome addition to the family. Ned was praying every night for a little brother. Finally, one time I told Ned, 'Ned I have some real good news for you.' And he said, 'What is that?' I said, 'Something you've been wanting for a long, long time.' And he said 'A monkey.' And I said, 'No, better than that, a little brother.'

"Mother and Daddy had a home down at Ocean Drive, and that's where we stayed in the summer time. When Hazel came along, that was 1954. Daddy was not well at the time, and when we heard about Hazel, he said, 'Well, one thing about it, I don't have to worry about our house because it was really well built. I had the best contractor we could possibly find and he took every precaution to make it sturdy.' So Ickie and Ned and I went down to see about it. Buddy was a little fellow then. The closer we got to our house, the more destruction had taken place. When we got to our spot there was very little standing there. There were two or three commodes sitting there that had been left, but the house had been washed out to another lot. So we took pictures to make Daddy believe it. We had to move the house because it was on someone else's lot. Ickie said, 'Daddy, if I take it down will you let me bring it back and put it out at the river?' because we had bought lot out at the river. So, Daddy and Ickie had the house taken apart and all the lumber brought back up here. Downstairs was destroyed completely, but the upstairs... and a funny thing the kitchen, when we opened the cabinets, some of the glasses and bottles that had been on the shelves, the Worchestershire sauce and the catsup and the condiments that had been on the shelf were still standing. The old GE refrigerator was on the lot. It had a coil on top. That was one way we could spot the lot. We brought it on up here, but Daddy did not live long enough to see the finished product. And it still smells just like the beach to me.

"My mother's name was Fannie. She was Fannie Friedham. My father's name was James Edward Marshall. Well of course my mother's parents were Sophie and Arnold Friedham, and my father's parents were Capt. J.W. Marshall and May Clausen Marshall from York.

"Getting back to my childhood, as children, we would play 'no bears out tonight,' and hopscotch out front, and we'd go play fox and hounds. You know, you'd go and hide. You'd drop little papers.

"Another thing we did as children, I think parents will appreciate this. The Dunlaps and the Twittys and the Marshalls were right close neighbors. We'd go to the Twittys and kind of edge around and see what they had for lunch, and then we'd come over here...and we'd end up at the place that had the best food. An interesting story, back to my childhood again. My brother Arnold was very inventive. The next door neighbor, Walter Dunlap, was the same way. So, they hooked up a little telephone with tin cans, and they had to run it from Arnold's room up to Walt's room, and they would carry on a conversation, like a walkie-talkie. We had to create our

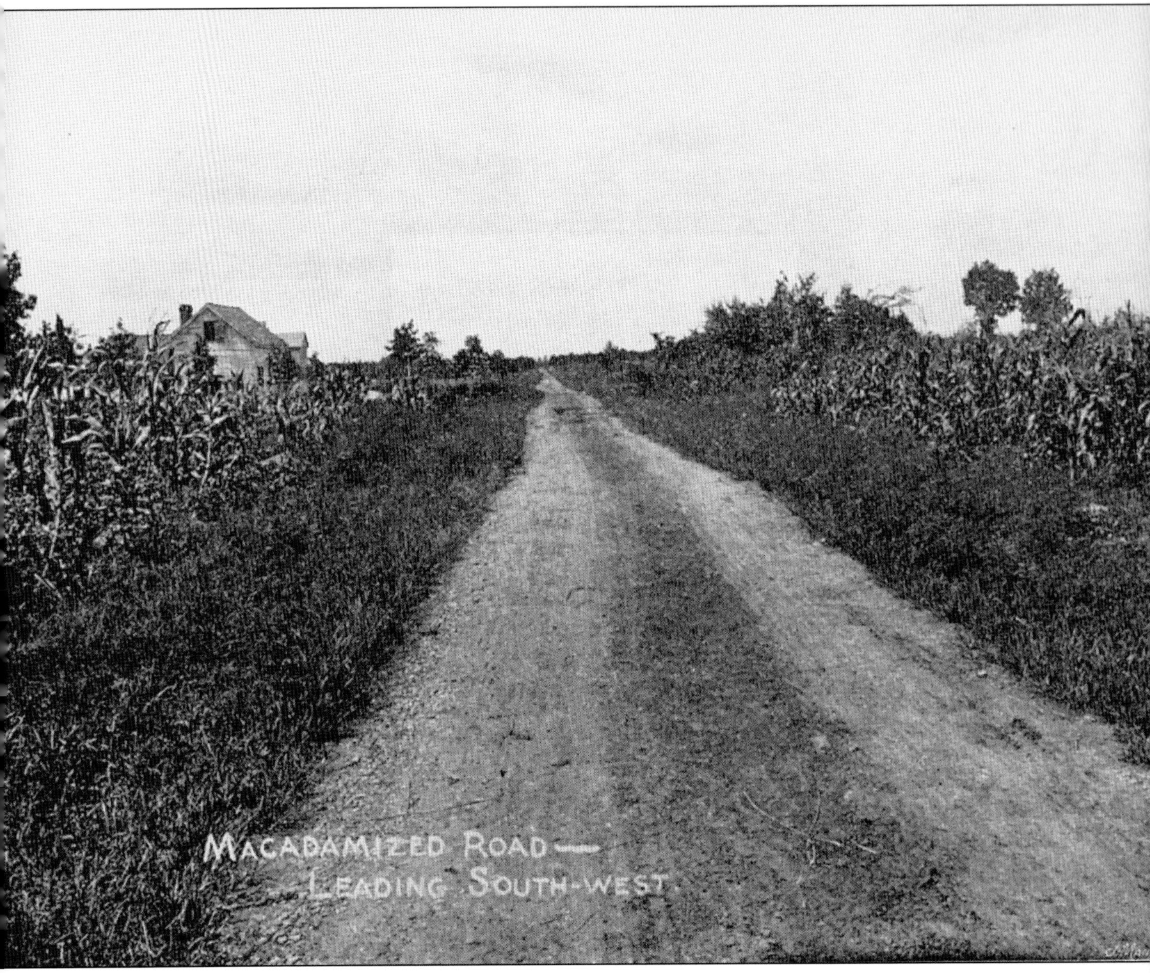

Farm and town were closely linked by highways.

own entertainment. The Dunlaps had an uncle, Uncle Bernie, who would save all his funny papers, and he'd send a whole batch of funny papers and we'd enjoy the funny papers.

"When my husband came to Rock Hill he was an architect, but that was 1929, just beginning the depression, and he had to find other work. When he went down to Columbia to get a job in the drafting room where he had worked for awhile and the man took him back in the back and there was not one soul down here. So he started working for the International Harvester Co., and he was working with them when we married. Daddy liked to keep his flock close by, so he said, "Ickie, I'll put you up in the hardware business if you'll consider coming to Rock Hill and settling here." So, that was after we were married.

"It used to be we knew everybody in Rock Hill, white and black, and I'll never forget our garden club went to Washington. Ann Anderson had married and moved to the Washington area. She invited our garden club to come up and see her, so we went up. Of course, we stayed in a hotel. Mary Phillips and Tom Gettys were in Washington about that time, and that was what instigated this trip. There were six or eight of us, and 'My Fair Lady' was playing, and we all wanted to go see it. Ann had invited us out to her house for dinner that night, and I'll never forget Eva Trammel

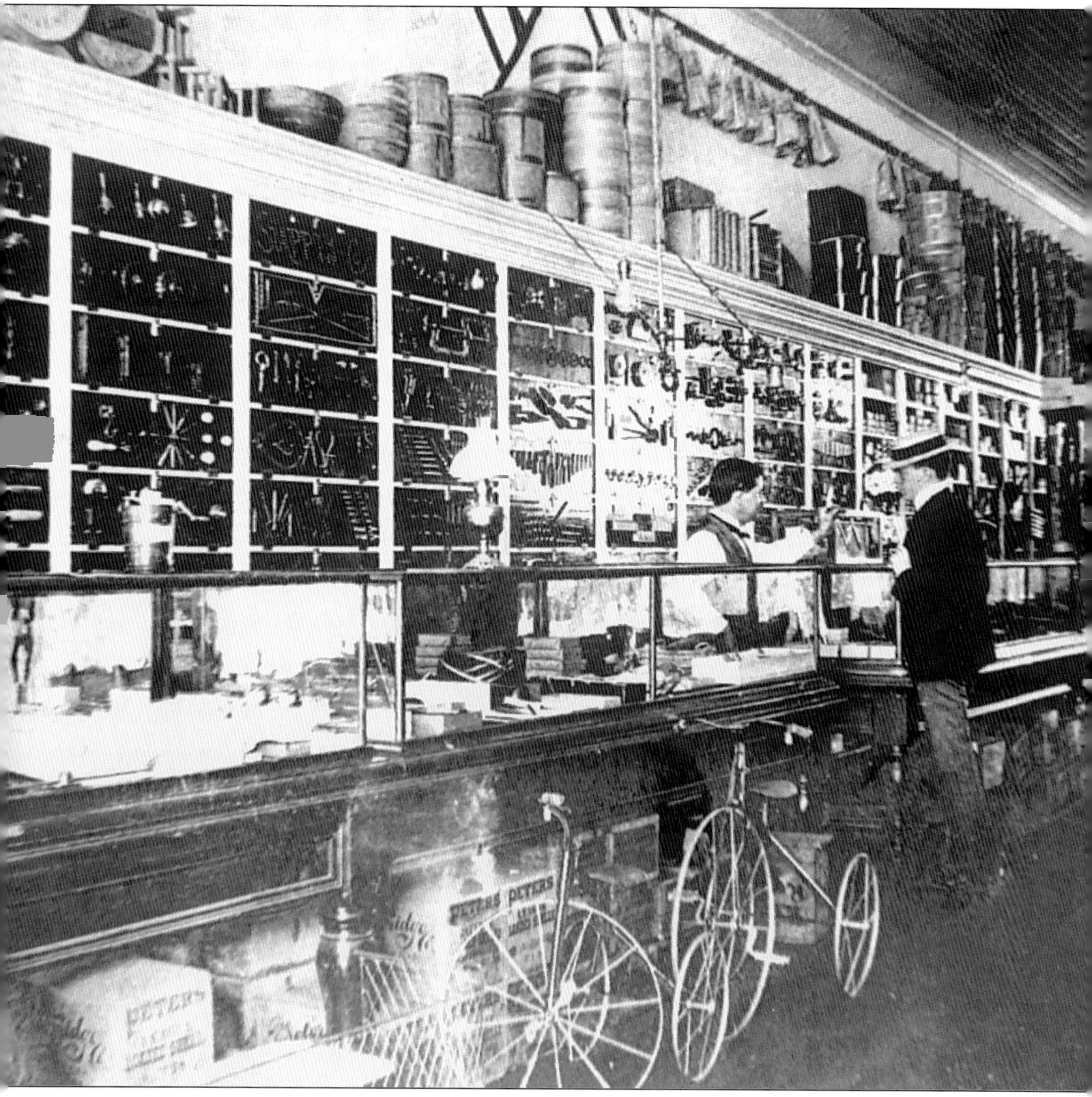

Downtown merchants offered everything from tricycles to saws to farm implements.

was along. Harlan Trammel's wife and he was head of Celanese at that time. We said something about going, and Ann said, 'You all can't go to that movie. It's in the wrong section of Washington.' And we all said, 'What do you mean we can't go?' Here we were from this little town that we thought we knew everybody and Celanese had come but we made a point to get to know everybody who worked for Celanese. She said it's not safe to go, and I said, 'You mean we're in our capital and it's not safe to go on the streets?' 'No, it isn't,' she said. And she said, 'You wouldn't walk down Black St. would you?' And I said, 'Certainly I'd walk down Black Street.' And I'd practically know everybody on the street. If I didn't know them, they'd know my Daddy. That was an awakening to me. I couldn't get over it.

"Here, there were several movie theaters. 'Stevenson' was there, and 'Old Majestic' was there, and I have to tell you a funny story. Mother wouldn't let us go to the movie on Saturday. She had her reasons, I'm sure, and good ones, but one of our friends, Louise Neely, had a birthday, and it happened to be on a Saturday. Her treat was to take us all to the movie. I guess there were eight or ten of us, all girls. All of a sudden they said, 'The movie is going to end here.' Ruth Rolland was on top of the train, and it was getting ready to go under a tunnel, and I said, 'It can't end here, it's not ending right.' And they said, 'It will carry on next Saturday and show what happens.' I never did get to see what happened to that poor woman!

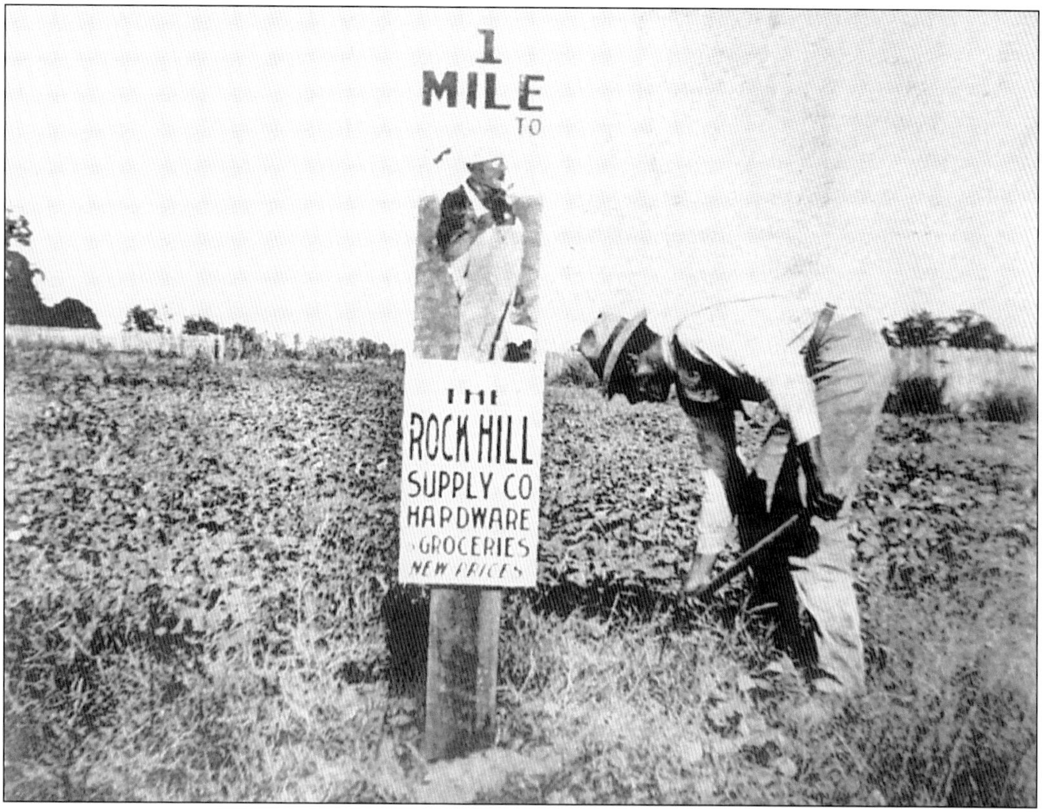

FIREBALLS AT CHRISTMAS

Farming communities such as Ogden were on the outskirts of Rock Hill. After the Civil War, African Americans found that while they had plenty of food produced by these farms, they lacked essential educational tools. Churches attempted to meet this need. In the following interview, two sisters, Rev. Marie Alexander and Mrs. Nancy Odom, recall the challenges of a new day in the history of our region.

"People would take the whole day and come to town when we were little girls. They would get some bricks, warm them up and get in the buggy. Our father was a farmer who raised cotton and corn. The land was good, called blackjack soil. He had a watermelon patch. He left a pair of shoes at the entrance to wear when he went in. The children put on shoes, took a watermelon and left the shoes in the same place as if headed out of the watermelon patch and went down to the back of the pasture to eat it.

"It was hot in the summers! There was a branch they went to and stayed in the water. Several families of children met at that branch. Our father made a fan by attaching newspapers to a board with the ends of the newspapers shredded. This, in turn, was attached to a stick. Father sat at the head of the dinner table and patted his foot to move the 'fan' back and forth over the table to cool and keep flies away.

"Living in the country, we had plenty to eat. I lived in Rock Hill to go to Emmett Scott one year. Father paid my tuition from his garden. I lived in the Castle Heights area and walked to school.

"Everybody played baseball. No gloves. You'd get yourself a stick of some kind and hit that ball. You'd make a ball from a rag, a stocking. If you wanted a hard ball, you'd wrap a rock.

"We started saving up before Christmas our cotton balls (picked bolls of cotton

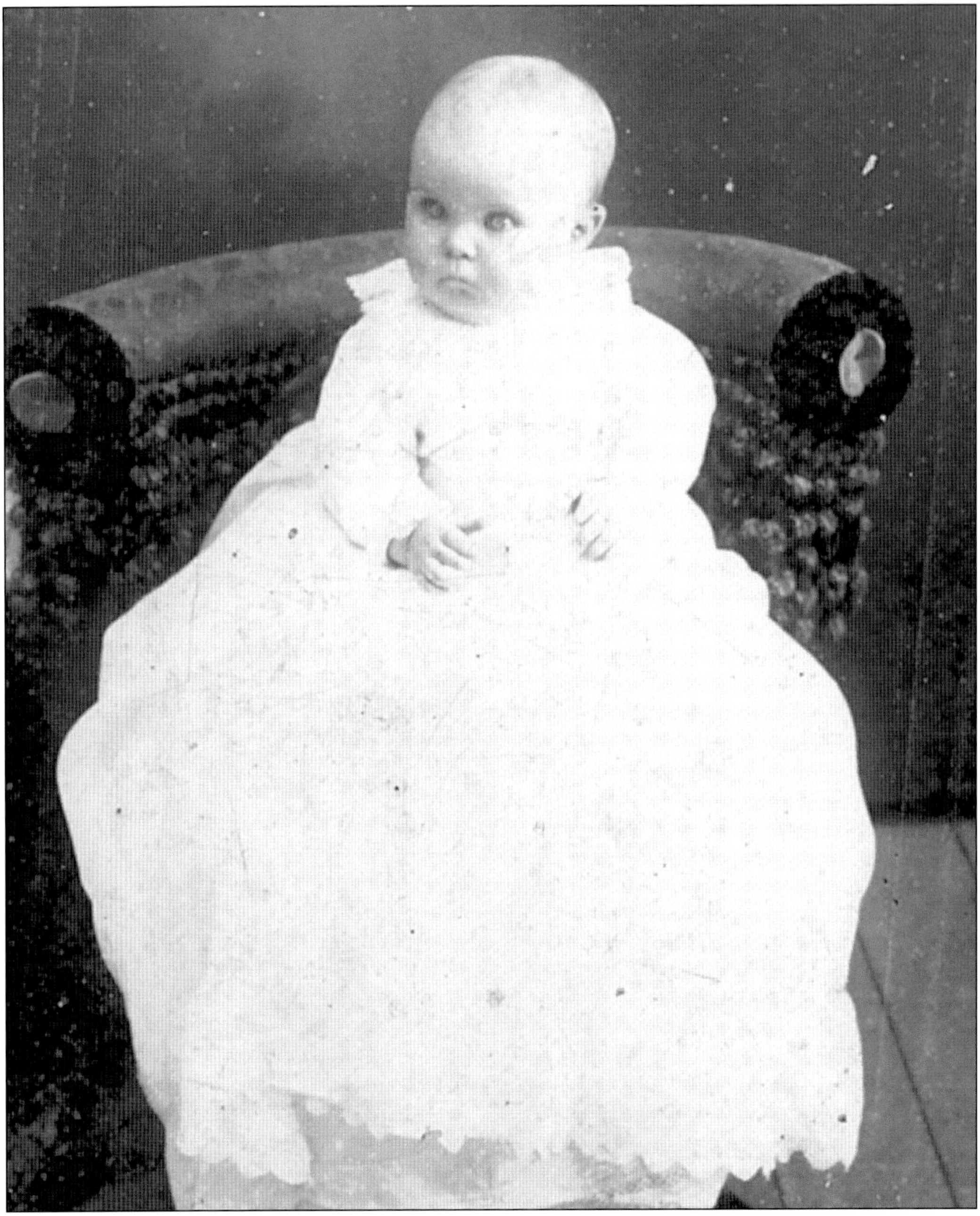

A Christmas dress is shown here, c.1905.

with seed) soaking them in Kerosene. Balls could be wrapped in layers for any size. At Christmas you lit them and threw them, but they set many things on fire. They were called fireballs. One Christmas it was warm, temperature in the 60s. All teenagers were at our cousin's house. They were throwing fire balls...at each other. I threw one which went down into a boy's overalls. Some boys buttoned them on the side, and others left them open. This particular one went down in front of the boy's overalls.

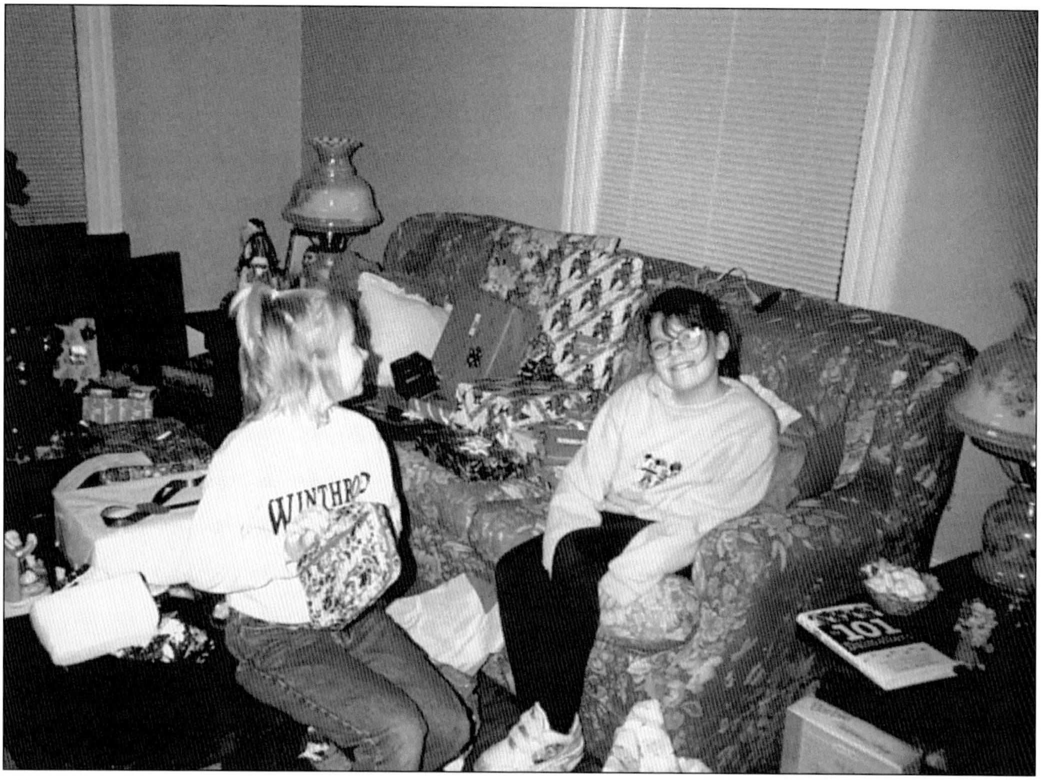

Christmas continues to be a special time of year.

He finally got it out. When I got home, my stepmother was so mad because I had kerosene all over my new dress! We made all our decorations. We went into woods to get holly and mistletoe to hang on the tree. Some people lit candles and put them on trees.

"Our family would have a turkey or a goose. Nearby relatives raised geese and turkeys. We cooked with all the trimmings on a big wood stove with a big water reservoir. We started baking cakes weeks before Christmas, wrapped them tightly in cloths and put them in a trunk, and they would stay moist til the holiday. We made pound cakes, a coconut cake, a chocolate cake, sometimes a fruitcake.

"We went to school in the country. All the churches had schools. Two rooms with all grades together. The churches had lodge halls where the men could meet. One school was a log cabin on someone's place. The children were in the front room where the fireplace was. Older children stayed in the kitchen. I don't know how we kept warm. The teacher would wear a dress a couple of days. Then, the next day, there'd be another dress on top of that one. What ever was left over from white schools around became our school books. A few had the back on, but most didn't.

"Most of the teachers were the preachers. They had gone to school at Friendship College. They and their wives mostly. If they went to the college most married a classmate. Methodists went to Clinton College. Most of the churches were Baptist. There was a Cedar Grove Methodist and a Cedar Grove Baptist. They still exist. The Presbyterian church is now gone. This is where our father went to school. His brother, Archie Johnson, taught them. Brothers were Johnny and Brown Johnson. Brown Johnson was the first black man to have anything to do with carrying the mail in Rock Hill. He

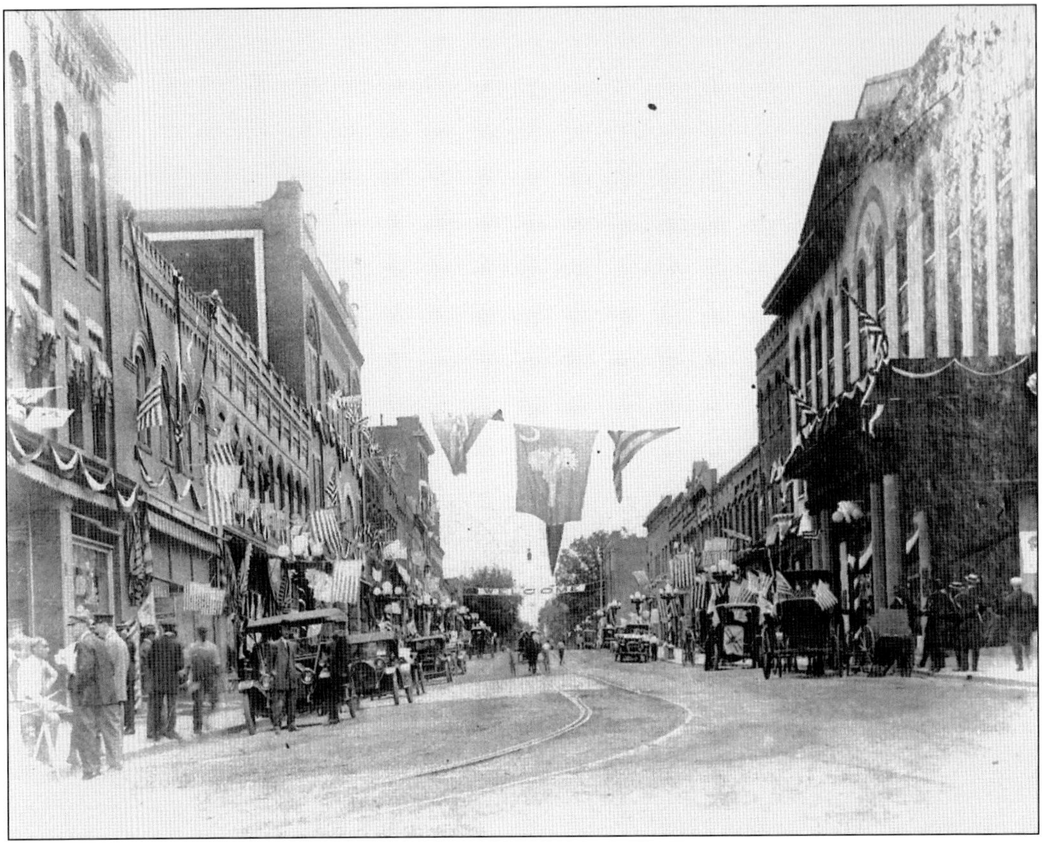

Independence Day provided an opportunity for farmers and city residents to celebrate.

took the mail from the station to the post office in his wagon. Later, his son did the same. All people who had any kind of education were taught by Uncle Archie.

"When slavery was over, three little girls were sent up to this area together. They did not want to separate them. They lived on the Bratton place. Some how, the Brattons were first cousins. Cousin Bob Bratton was a preacher. Cousin Sallie Hardin and Pearl Guthrie. Cousin Pearl married a Guthrie; whether he was white or black I don't know. But I do know that Bratton was white, and these other first cousins were half white.

"We have seen a lot. Just up the street was a well on the corner with a trough. When people came into town from the country, they would pull over for horses to drink and for the people to rest. Horses would, without prompting, pull in. There was also a much larger well on what was Trade Street, now David Lyle Boulevard."

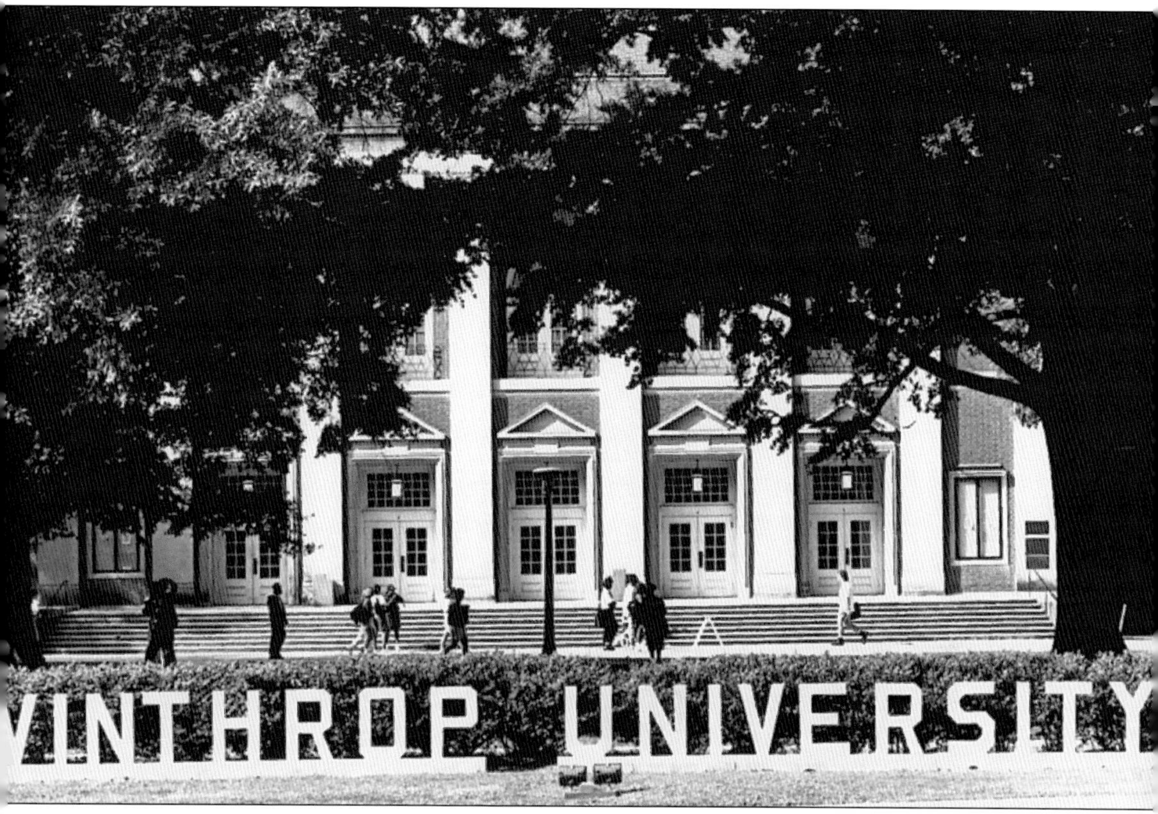

PARTNERS

In the mid-1890s, Benjamin Ryan Tillman, South Carolina's most powerful politician, formed a partnership with David Bancroft Johnson, the visionary first president of Winthrop College. Both men grasped the importance of creating an institution in the state's upcountry for the education of women. Thus, these two men forged an alliance that took a small Columbia school and built it into what is, today, a respected coeducational university.

Since the laying of the cornerstone of Main Building (Tillman Hall) over 100 years ago, both Rock Hill and Winthrop have complemented each other. They have strengthened one another from the first day; the city benefited from the institution's intellectual stimulation. And, of course, the college was granted a permanent home in the fertile soil of a diverse New South city. Since Tillman and Johnson became partners in 1894, town and campus have grown together. As University historian Ross Webb explains, "Winthrop University and the city of Rock Hill have been intertwined since the college moved to Rock Hill in 1895. Each has sustained the other in many ways. While the university has impacted both the society and economy of Rock Hill, the city has supported the university as it seeks to meet the needs both of the community and the state." Here, Winthrop archivist Ron Chepesiuk recounts the birth of the partnership in which no one loses and both Rock Hill and Winthrop take pride.

"By 1890, Winthrop had outgrown its Columbia facilities, forcing the college's board of trustees to consider finding a new home for the school. In July of that year, Dr. Edward Joynes made a speech in Florence in which he advocated that the Winthrop Training School be offered to the state for support.

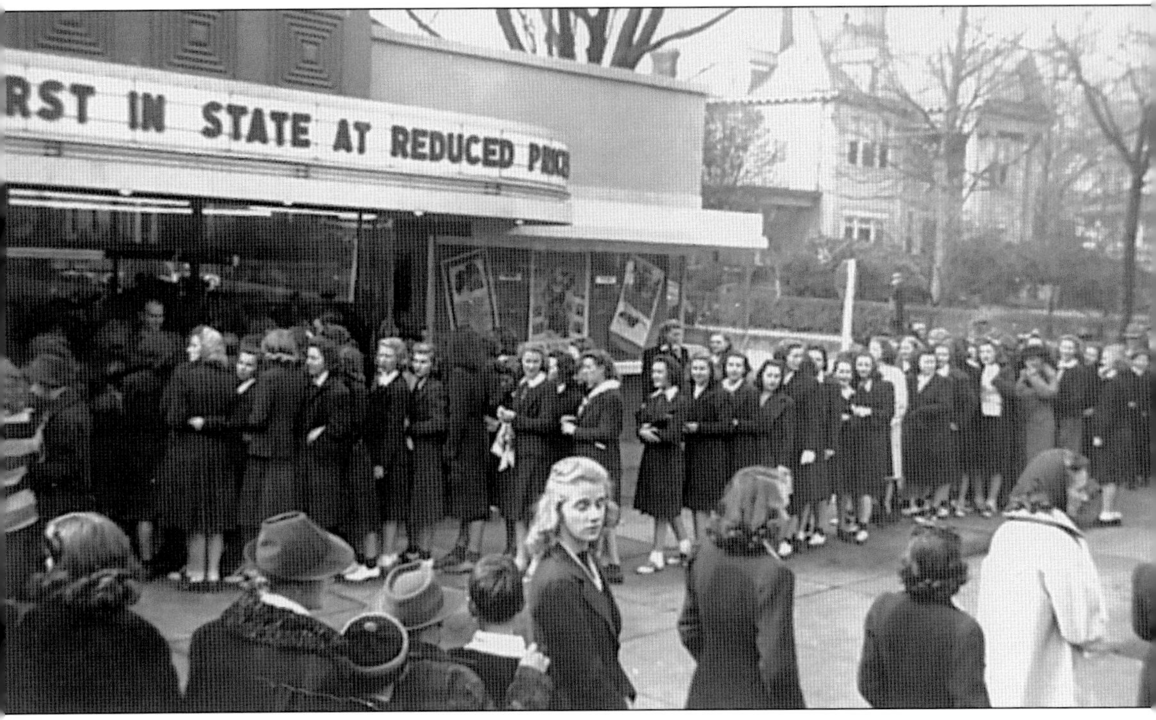

Winthrop students line up at the Pix Theater to view Gone With The Wind *in 1941.*

"Governor Ben Tillman was enthusiastic about the idea and, at Joynes's suggestion, appointed a committee to investigate costs and locations. In November 1891, the committee 'endorsed the union of industrial and normal training and recommended that an act be passed providing for the foundation of a State Industrial and Normal College for Women.'

"On December 23, 1891, the state ratified the act establishing the South Carolina Industrial and Normal College. On the same day, the legislature elected a board of trustees for the college and stipulated that the governor serve as chairman of the board. The legislature also authorized the use of 100 convicts to work as laborers for the construction of the college's buildings.

"One of the first actions of the newly elected board of trustees was to open bids to South Carolina cities that wanted to serve as a site for the college. Advertisements were placed in state newspapers for 30 days. When the board met in March 1892, the only cities to make offers were Anderson and Columbia. At first, Anderson's bid seemed the more attractive of the two— an offer of $75,000 plus land to build on —but a court ruled the city's bonds invalid. After bids were reopened, Rock Hill and Spartanburg became the leading contenders.

"Since the board was having difficulty choosing between the two, it decided to visit each city in order to make the proper decision. Unfortunately for Spartanburg, the board's visit coincided with the laying of the cornerstone of Converse College, an event which, undoubtedly, influenced the board's decision.

"Rock Hill's bid showed strong community support for the new college. In a referendum, an overwhelming 273 of 297 ballots favored a bond issue of $60,000. Eager to attract the college, Rock Hill also offered a choice of two sites.

"When the ten members of Winthrop's board of trustees met on April 2, 1893, their sentiments were clear—eight votes for Rock Hill and two for Spartanburg.

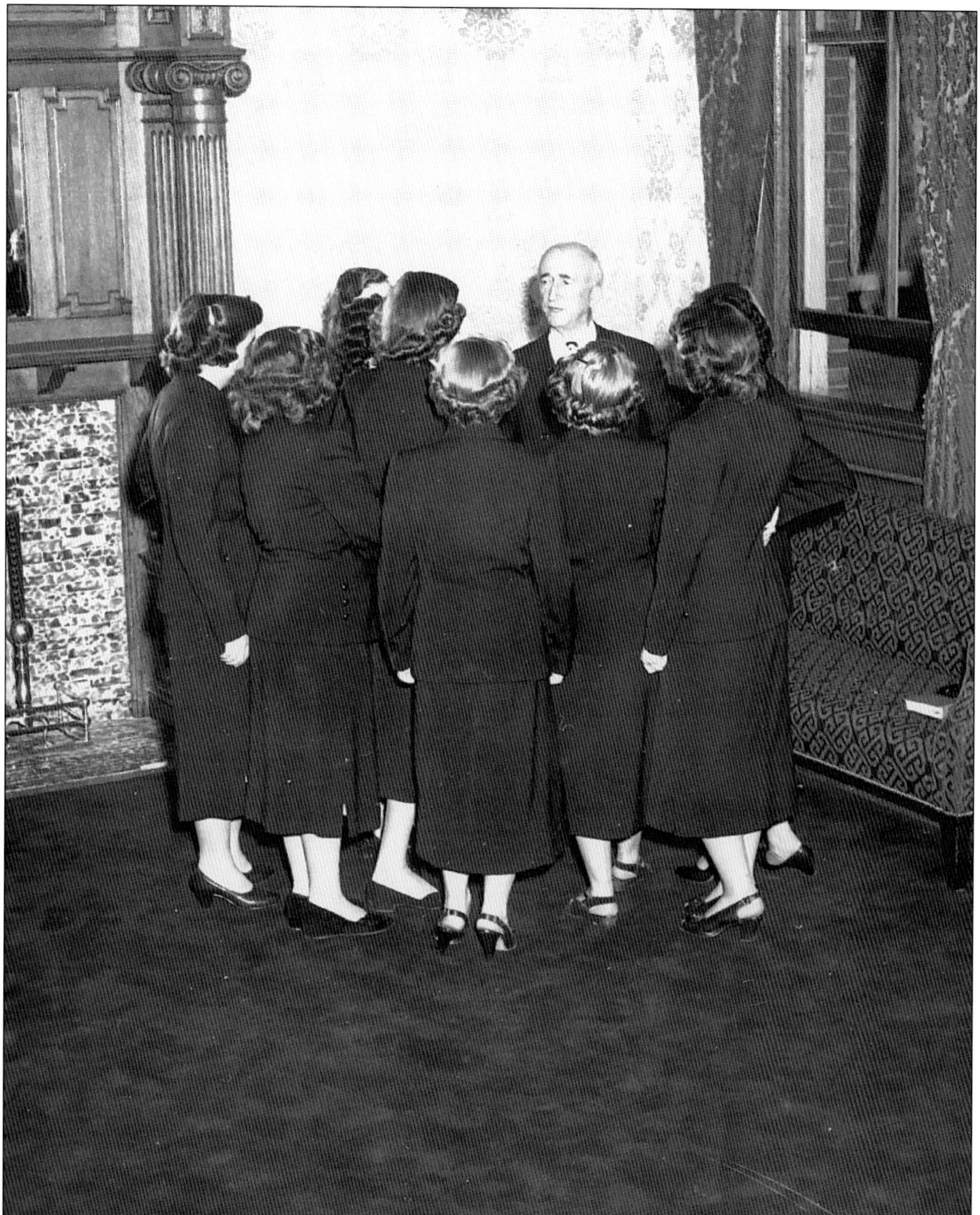

Governor James F. Byrnes chats with a group of students in the early 1950s.

"Triumphant in its efforts to attract Winthrop College, the town celebrated jubilantly. As bells rang and factory whistles blew, a band led more than a 1,000 townsfolk in a victory march through the city.

"A delegation from Winthrop's board visited Rock Hill on June 1, 1893, to settle details about the bonds and the site for the college. Sixty bonds of $1,000 each were deposited in the Rock Hill First National Bank, and the Oakland site was chosen as

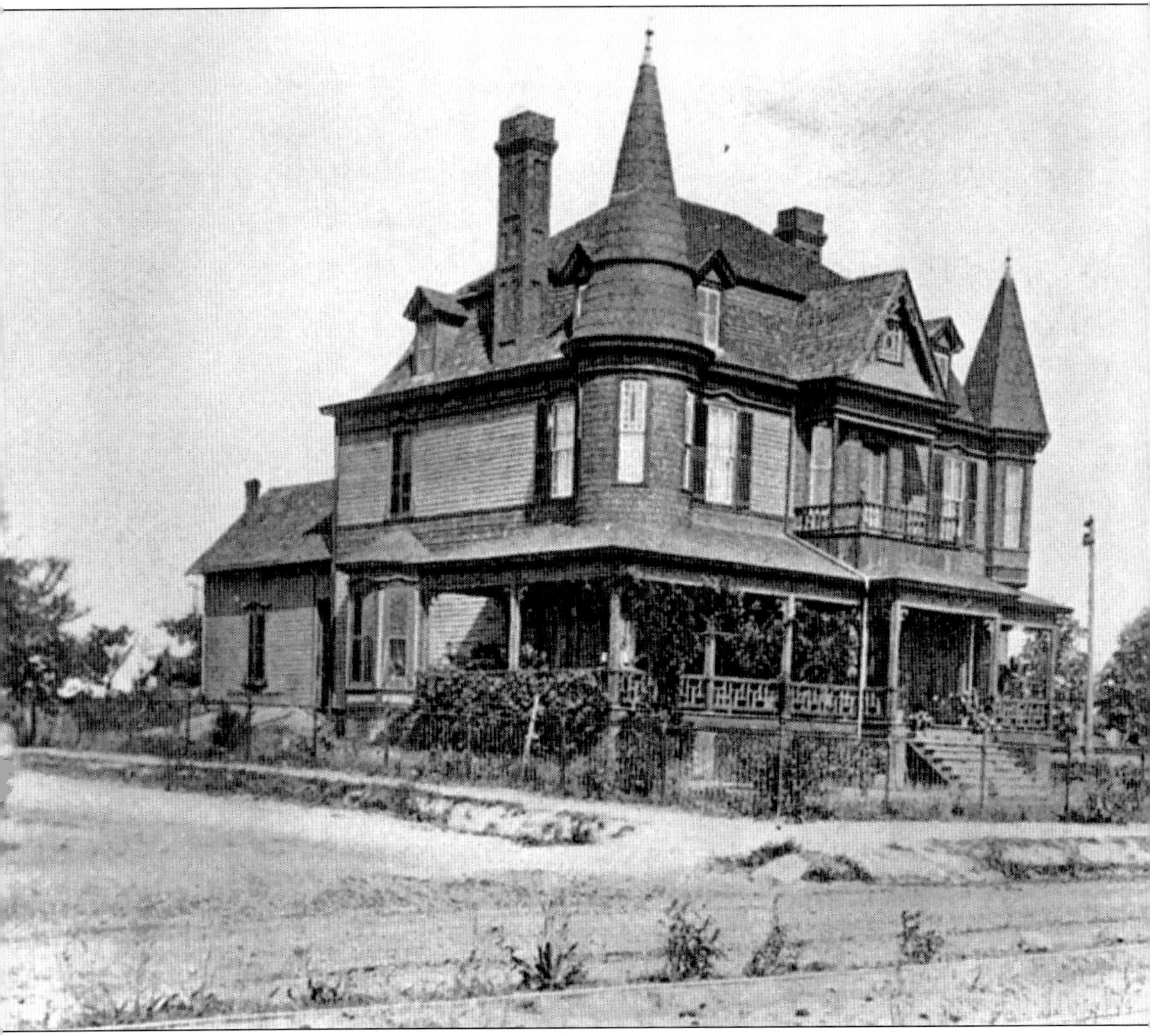

Here is the president's house on Oakland Avenue, c.1900.

the college's future home. Two Rock Hill businessmen, Dr. T.A. Crawford and W.J. Roddey, were then elected trustees.

"With the site chosen, the board moved quickly to build the campus. The Atlanta firm of Burne and Morgan, which had designed the Clemson campus in 1891, was selected to design the first building.

"On May 12, 1894, the birthday of Robert C. Winthrop, festivities for the laying of the cornerstone of Winthrop's impressive new Main Building took place. Robert C. Winthrop, unable to attend because of poor health and advancing years, wished the new college well, saying 'May it continue to be, for centuries to come, an ornament and a support to the state which has so wisely and liberally funded it.'

"At 9 a.m. marshals started to assemble in the streets. An estimated 10,000 spectators came from all corners of the state. Trains brought the entire Clemson student body.

"At noon the official ceremony began in front of the Main Building. Ira D. Jones, speaker of the South Carolina House of Representatives, praised the educational progress of the state as mirrored in Winthrop's rapid development. Governor Tillman then

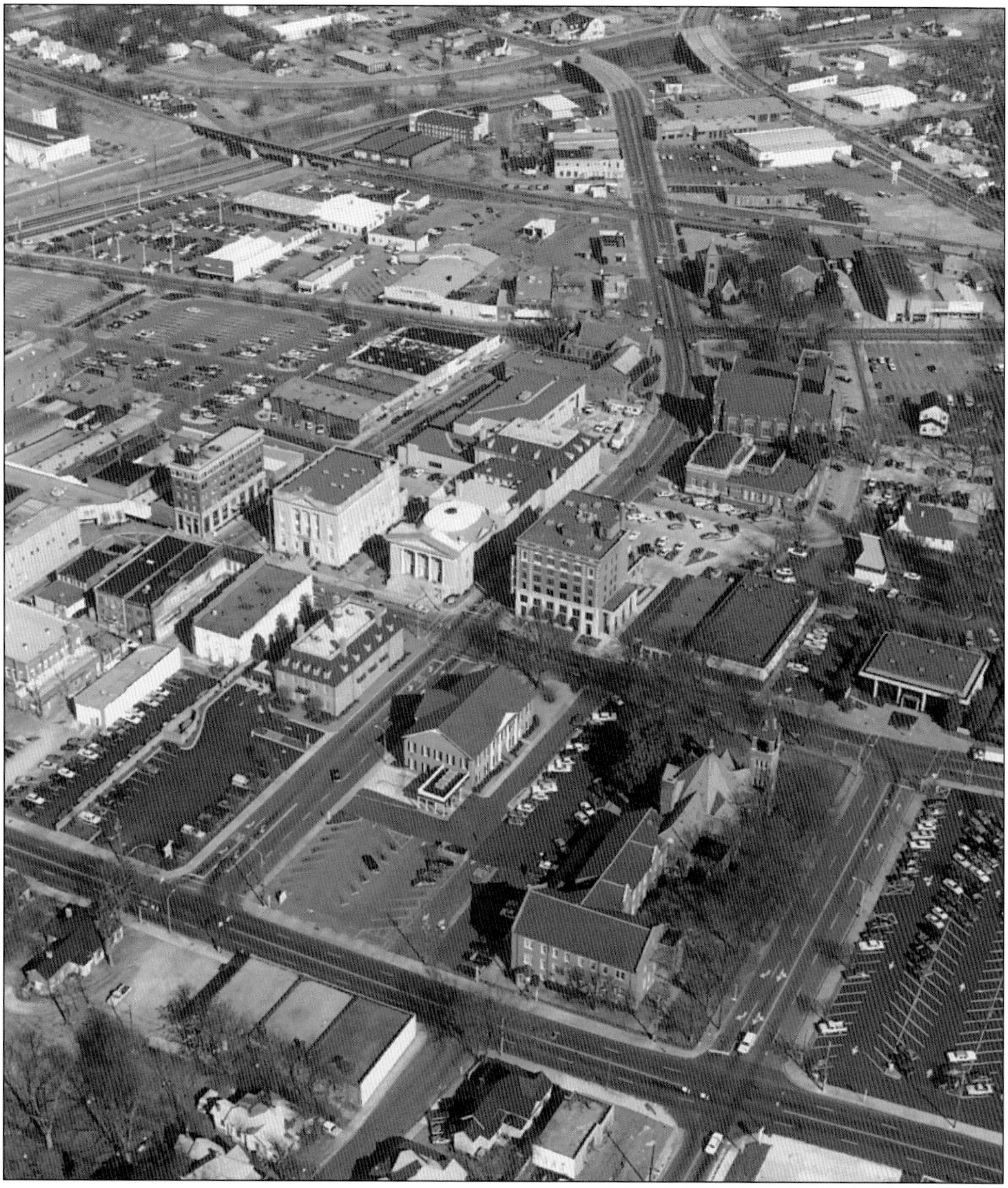

Shown here is an aerial photograph of downtown Rock Hill in 1988.

observed the historic date: 'We have met to celebrate with fitting ceremonies the laying of the cornerstone of this state institution of learning.'

"At 1 p.m., a hushed silence fell as workmen lowered the cornerstone at the east front corner of the new building. As the stone nestled into place, a crescendo of cheers rose.

"There was a feeling throughout the state that this was an important day in South Carolina history. *The State* newspaper, in an editorial typical of South Carolina newspapers, wrote:

"'This day marks the opening of an era of state aid in the education of women in South Carolina. It is an era of which all may be proud and may join in the celebration

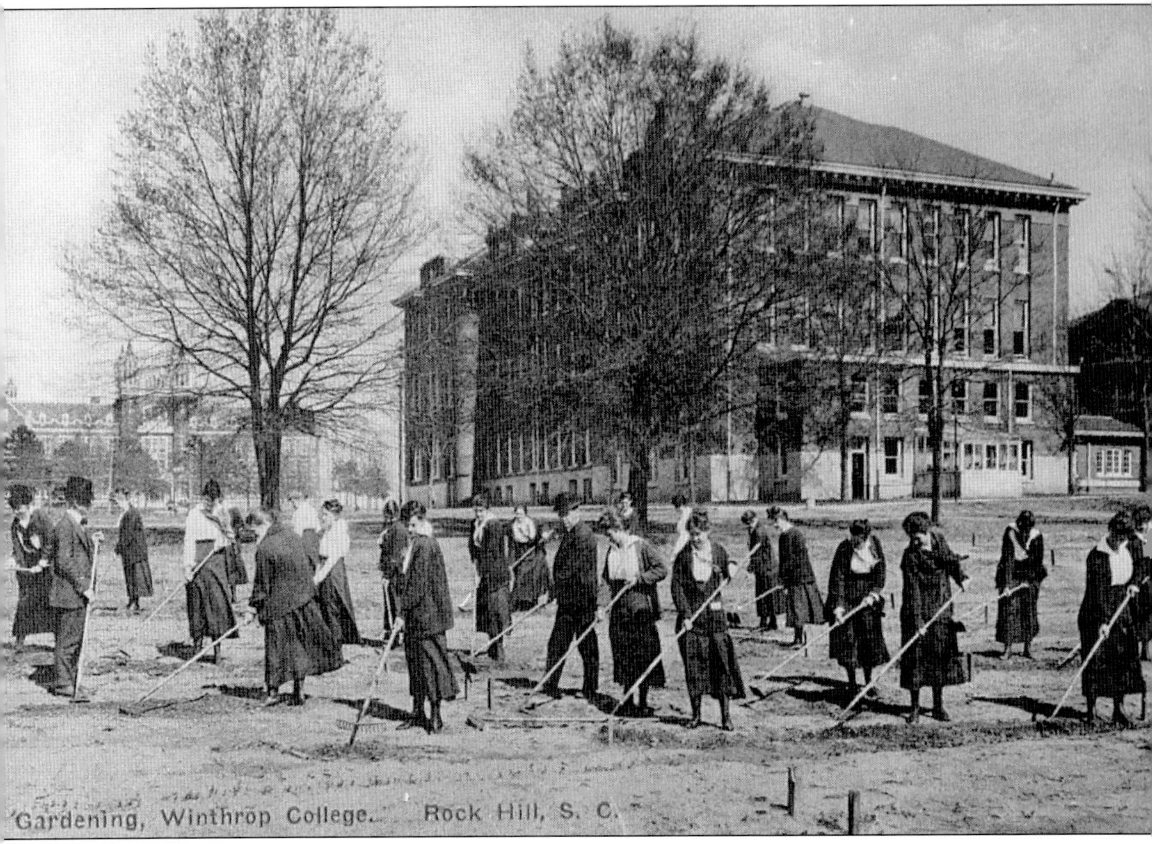

Students enrolled in a gardening class in the early 1900s.

of its inauguration. Heretofore, the state has devoted its money to the education of its men. But now...it says that women of South Carolina must no longer grow up in ignorance because they are poor.'"

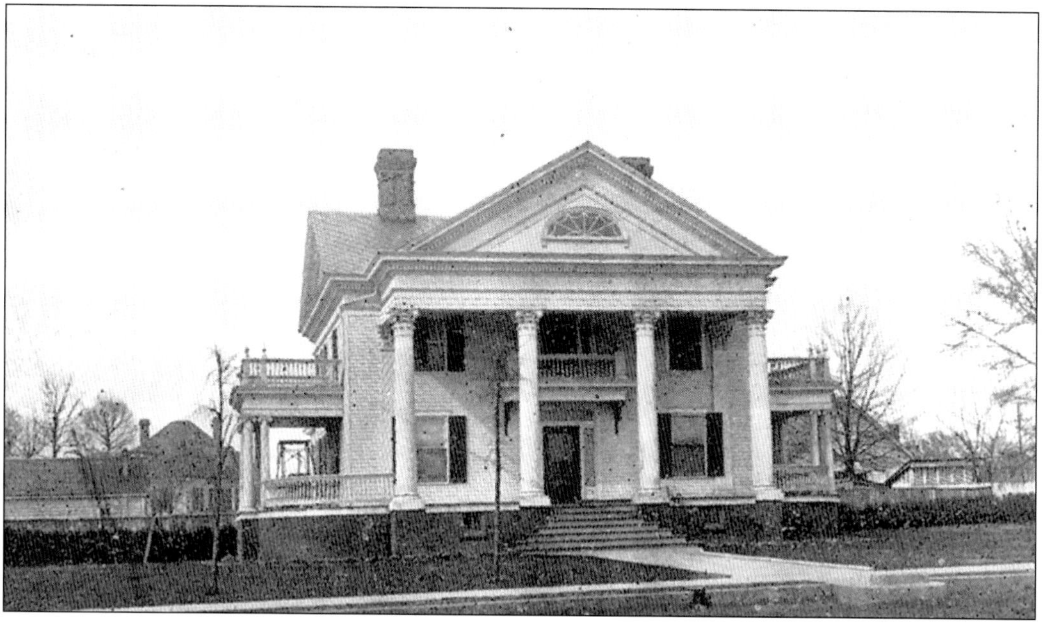

Cooperation

The artery which connects downtown to Winthrop University is Oakland Avenue. The matriarch of one of Rock Hill's oldest families was the late Addie Stokes Mayfield, the daughter of an early Rock Hill dentist. Born early this century, Mrs. Mayfield recalled the mules "Elec" and "Tric" that powered the streetcar which operated under a canopy of luscious trees along Oakland Avenue. Her home, built from 1906 to 1907, remains a stellar example of neoclassical architecture with a two-story portico and heart of pine floors imported from Colleton and Hampton Counties.

Mrs. Mayfield's life spanned most of the twentieth century, including a lengthy teaching career that began upon her graduation from Winthrop College in 1937. She was a "town girl," living just down Oakland Avenue from the campus. Like other students of the Great Depression, she found that "everyone was in the same boat." Here, Mrs. Mayfield reflects on the changes that she witnessed from her Oakland vantage point. "The key has been," Mrs. Mayfield stresses, "cooperation."

"Oakland Avenue was a cotton field at one time. This early picture shows that, because the trees were just little sprouts. All the big trees had finally died of old age, and they had planted three elms on one side of this lot and three elms on the other. They all succumbed to the elm blight that went through, except for one on the end that's still there. It's in pretty bad shape. It's a broad-leaf elm and it was not susceptible to the blight. My parents said they had to plant chinaberry trees to have any shade. They grew fast, and they put two on each side. By the time I was able to climb trees, I think I came along about ten years after the house was built, the leaves, the branches were just beautiful. They were low and big, and a child could walk up them almost. It was just great for climbing.

"This house was built in 1906. Actually they started in 1906, and I think it was finished up in the spring of 1907. About six months. What happened was my father's father was in the lumber, sawmill business, down about 50 miles from Charleston, and they had a lot of virgin pine. He had a rice plantation, and after the Civil War, he

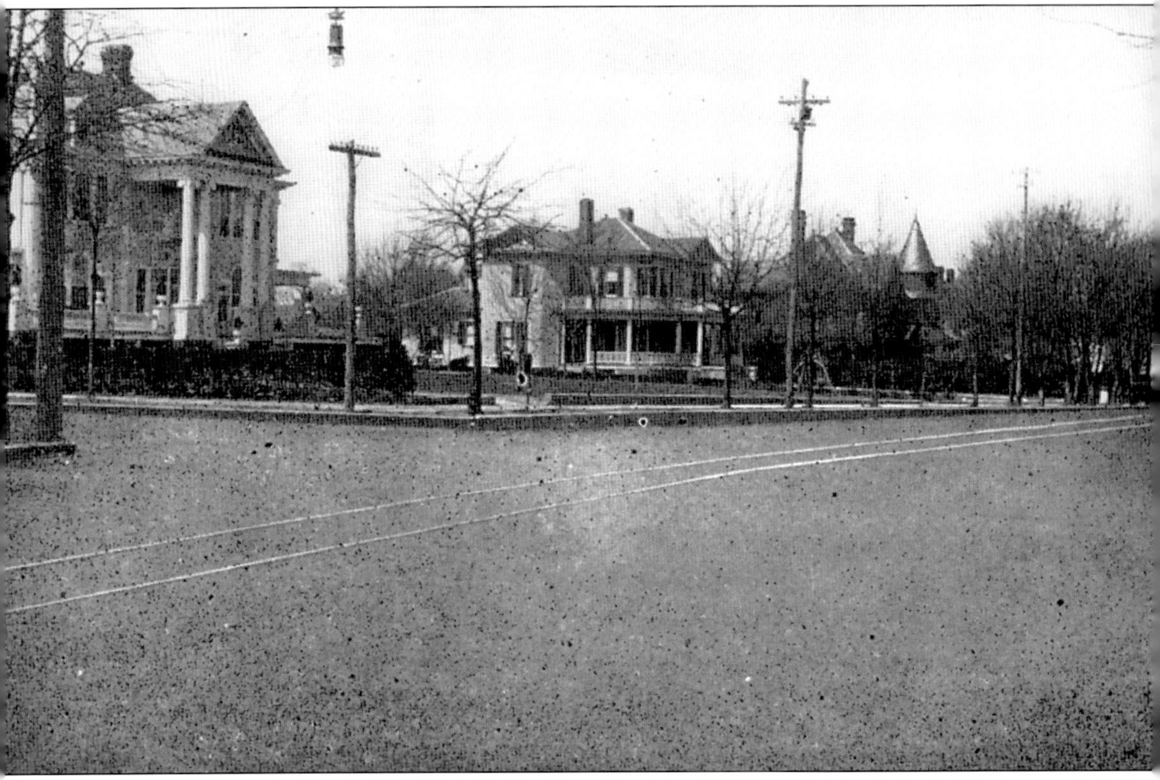

had fought all through the war up in the Virginia area and started out in S.C., but then they moved the whole group up into the Virginia area for about two years, and he wrote home every day. He apparently had no prejudice at all. He was a pragmatist. He had the land, and a Yankee partner had the money, and he went into the sawmill business after the war with a Yankee.

"And they were as good friends as they could be. I think his name was Settlemyer. So that's where the lumber for this house came from. All of it was built of heart of pine lumber from about 50 miles from Charleston. It was Colleton County and part of the plantation was in Hampton County. They could not grow rice without the cheap slave labor. Of course it wasn't so cheap in the long run. Then my mother had some stock she sold, and they put in in this house. So they started off, and they said for 25 years, they didn't have to do a thing to the house. It just held up great. You know it was well built and good materials. Then they said for the next 25 years, they didn't do anything but repair it.

"They kept it up. Then when my husband and I got it, we kept it up. It never has been restored for the simple reason we have always been interested in keeping it just like it always was. There must have been ten houses, built in this style, right straight down Oakland Avenue all the way to Main Street.

"This street was elegant. It was beautiful, and as it got into the 1930s, it really was pretty where those early trees were big and overlapped the street they made a canopy over Oakland. It really was pretty. Now they've gone ahead and put out these trees again, and I suppose one day it will be pretty again. The main thing that ruined these big houses for the second generation was the paint. You know, they put lead in the paint to make it stick. Actually, my folks said if you started at one side, before you really got around, unless you had a big crew, that it was already washing off. There was no way you could keep these painted,

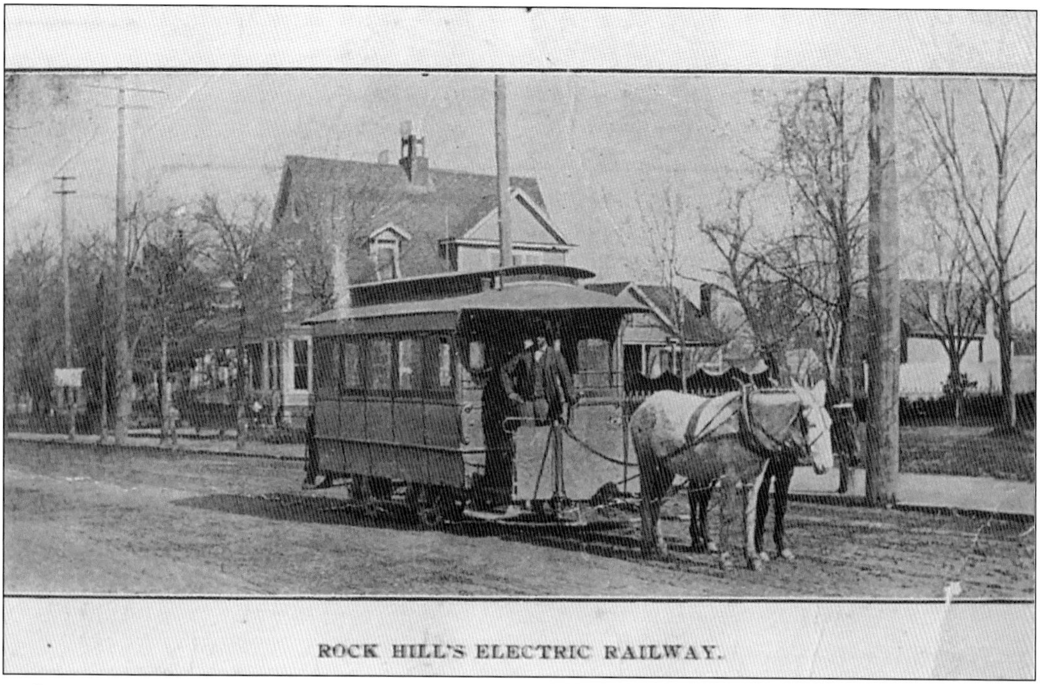

"Elec" and "Tric" transported travelers from Oakland to Main Street.

and it was not worth it to people, and they just let them go down. They rented them to tenants who took even less interest. But then the third generation tried their best to restore what was left. Now, I think, that the Andersons and our family were the only ones of the second generation who were so interested in history that we did keep our houses up.

"The Gills, part of the Anderson family, have done a wonderful job, and it was really sort of like this house. It never was too bad off. It was green, and it wasn't as pretty as it is now. But, it's beautiful now. Now that bunch was older than my parents. It was built about 1890.

"I remember when they took the street car tracks up. I was about six years old, I think, and they...you know about the 'electricity'...the mules they named 'Elec' and 'Tric.' There's a great big stone out in our side yard. Two or three men brought it out to our side yard when they dug up the tracks, so they could pave Oakland. And the property owners had to pay for them to pave Oakland. It wasn't anything like a state highway then, so everyone had to pay their prorata share. It was so well done that I don't remember them ever having to restore that road out there. I really don't. The streetcar started there at Cherry Road past Winthrop and went straight on down to East Main.

"I honestly don't remember riding on the streetcar. I would have been old enough to, certainly, as a pre-school child, but I don't remember riding on a streetcar. But I do remember the tracks being taken up, and the rock is still in our side yard that they pulled out of the road when they took the tracks up.

"It was drawn by mules, and they first tried the electric system because they had it in 1905, I think. Duke Power got electricity, and actually, it just didn't work. It was unsatisfactory. It would go a little bit and stop, in a most inconvenient time. So they put the mules back. I think they maybe had started out with mules and then converted, then went back to mules, so they named them 'Elec' and 'Tric.' I thought that was real cute.

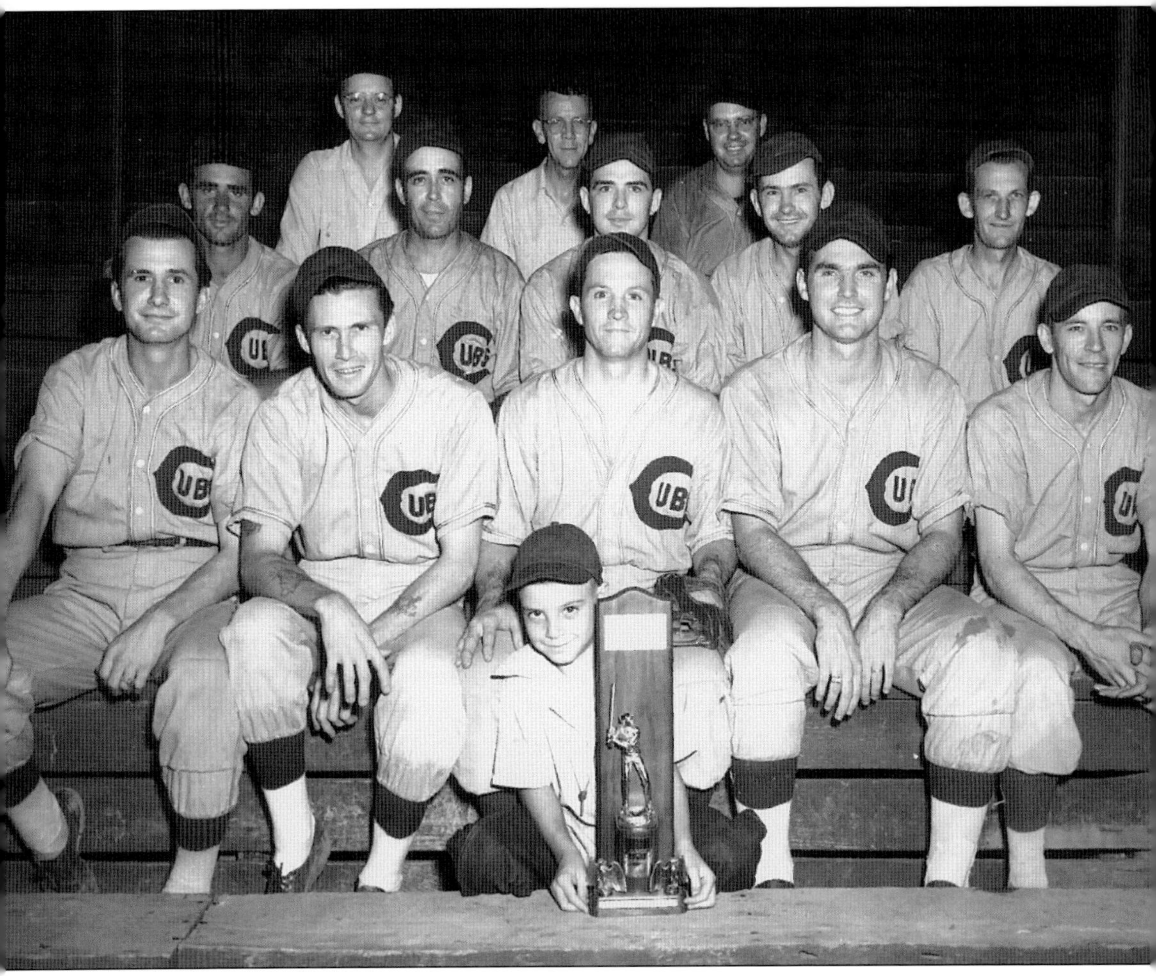

The Bleachery softball team is pictured here in 1947.

"In the late thirties everybody was strapped for cash. I remember that, you know we wore uniforms at Winthrop, but town girls just had to wear anything blue, navy, or white or black, and I remember I had two dresses that weren't uniforms, two Sunday dresses. But nobody minded because everybody was in the same boat. There was no cash anywhere. I remember when I was in the tenth or ninth grade... You know how things impress you as a child, and you wonder why, but I guess this would impress anybody. But I remember the sun was streaming in that front door, and my daddy was coming downstairs from the bedroom. We all slept upstairs then. He said, 'Addie, all the money I've got in the world is in my hip pocket. The bank closed and a lot of people think it may never reopen.' That was in 1932, when we had the bank holiday. Sure enough, the bank did close, and it never did reopen. They said it paid out less than a third of the people's deposits, which was about par for the course. People's Bank never did close.

"I went to teach in '37–'38. I was 21 years old. So I went down to Walterboro and just loved it, and the people were absolutely the nicest things. If there was a dance at the Country Club, they saw that the teachers got dates to go, you know, introduced them to people. I never saw anything like it. I never saw anything like the hospitality. I've always loved the upcountry, but I noticed a certain amount of hospitality and something down there that is indefinable. They just were that way. I don't know whether every Lowcountry town would be that way.

"I thought it was wonderful, and my father had been reared just 50 miles from there. He wasn't reared in a town. He was reared on a plantation. They named this plantation 'Early' for a very famous Confederate general that he thought so much of, his father thought so much of. They called it 'Early Branch,' and I think it was more or less in Hampton County, more of it in Hampton County than in Colleton County, and then when he went into the lumber business, I think he swapped some of the Hampton land for some pine lands in Colleton County...I have seen the place one time, but the house burned, so when there's no house there, it's hard to get the definition of how things were. But down there when we went that time, must have been in the fifties, the long-leaf pine, virgin, was still standing, a whole lot of it down there. And then we went back again, and it had all been cut down. This was in the sixties. Those trees, those old pines, high things, cut.

"My husband and I married here in '43, but we went right to Atlanta. That was during the war, and my husband was in war work. He had a bad left eye and was classified as 4-F. So he had to go to work at Bell Aircraft. He was in the personnel department until we came back here. He was there, and they had put him in charge of sales of surplus equipment. Then he went into the furniture business with Maxwell Brothers. Maxwell Brothers changed stores, and they offered him a partnership with the three Maxwell Brothers. Fortunately, Maxwell Brothers' store here, Mr. Moore wanted to sell out and be independent of them, so they put him in Rock Hill. So it was an accident that we got back to Rock Hill. This was Mr. Jim Moore. You know Moore Furniture that is still here? He was with Maxwell Bros. It was where George Dunlap's Building and Loan was. That building was torn down. It's a Building and Loan now, but it was a furniture store. That was Maxwell-Mayfield for 18 years. Then we went into the first payroll business in the south. That sounds pretentious, but people didn't go into the payroll business. It's become very ordinary, and the ones that are so big now were younger than we are. We went into it in 1960, and we've been in it ever since. My son runs it now.

"Rock Hill in the late 1950s and early 1960s was a nice town. I don't notice much difference then and now except for the fact it was more social, just pure social life. Not clubs and things but people just giving parties.

"You know, I don't know whether you know it or not, but I wrote a little book on Rock Hill. See that little blue book under the table? A bunch of dentists, a committee of dentists, asked me to write a history of dentistry in Rock Hill, and I told them I would try to do it. My father was a dentist. And I said, nobody will read it unless you let me put some Rock Hill history as a background. So I said, 'I'll be glad to try.' So after much discussion, we decided that we would make at least a third, sometimes two-thirds of the six chapters, on the history of Rock Hill and stay with the art of dentistry at that period in history. Then the other part would be biographical of all the dentists. I don't think we missed a one, because if they had been dead, I went over to Laurelwood Cemetery and looked at the stones, found when they died, and then found their obituary in the *Herald.* That was easy when you could find the obituary. That was as good as you wanted. So we did, we have the living and all who every practiced dentistry up to Desert Storm. There is a good bit of Rock Hill history in it.

"As I mentioned, I was a day student at Winthrop. This will surprise you. I think I got my education for $75 a semester. And the textbooks were rental. And if you took care of them, you didn't have to pay anything. See, I went in '34 and went through til '37. That was the depth of the Depression. Because the stock market had crashed in '29. I remember when I got in the Book and Q. That was something you loved to get into. I didn't buy a Q. It cost $5. That was a lot of money for something just to hang on a charm bracelet.

"I found that, people always ask you, what did you find that was true of the history of Rock Hill. The main thread I saw running though this history as I researched my book was that there were never any wealthy, not really any wealthy, people in Rock Hill.

"The only way that we got where we got, and it has been a great little town. It's done things. We have all worked hard. Listen, Winthrop made Rock Hill and Rock Hill made Winthrop. Because Rock Hill opened its arms and its pocketbooks, and Winthrop put Rock Hill on a different footing. The ones that did not have an education, got an education. Well, you know you don't come out the same way if you've been educated for two and three and four generations. It's been a partnership. But what I was going to tell you that there weren't wealthy people, but they always managed. They might argue, but they always managed to agree before it was over. They got Winthrop, and the first steam-driven cotton mill and the bleachery. Everything was done by cooperation in this city.

"And our people had the drive and the ambition. And the first steam mill that we got here they even sold stock to school children. Everybody had a part in getting the first cotton mill, and there are five or six illustrations like that. I really think it's remarkable, how we've cooperated.

A Small World

Main Street has gone through several incarnations. In the 1930s and 1940s, the business district was bracketed by stately homes on East and West Main Streets. As the economy changed, attempts were made to revitalize the commercial section, but landmarks such as Friedham's Department Store closed in the early 1960s. A covered mall proved unsuccessful, and in 1994, the roof was removed.

Through all of the changes, Mrs. Vera Pursley has enjoyed her East Main Street home. She has witnessed the steady arrival of new people to Rock Hill, the exodus of young men to fight in wars, the closing of the textile mills, and the rise of Rock Hill Printing and Finishing. Through all of the changes—in business and in social composition—she cherishes growing up in "a small world."

"East Main was a beautiful street. It had beautiful trees. The trees met in the middle of the street, and you were close to town. You were close to church. You were close to the bank, and some of the grocery stores were down Main Street. It was just convenient.

"And Oakland Avenue was a beautiful street. You know, it had those big trees, and they met like a canopy. Some of the old homes up there have been torn down. The Mayfield House, thank goodness, is still standing, and that's one of the prettiest houses up there.

"I've known Addie Mayfield all my life. I went to Winthrop Training School. Her sister was in a class with me. Rock Hill was so different. I was thinking the other day, you knew everybody. There was a lot of entertaining going on, a lot of teas and receptions. And you dressed up. Women wore hats and kid gloves back then. We really dressed up.

"We used to have a lot of parades in Rock Hill. I don't remember what all we had parades for, but we had it when the

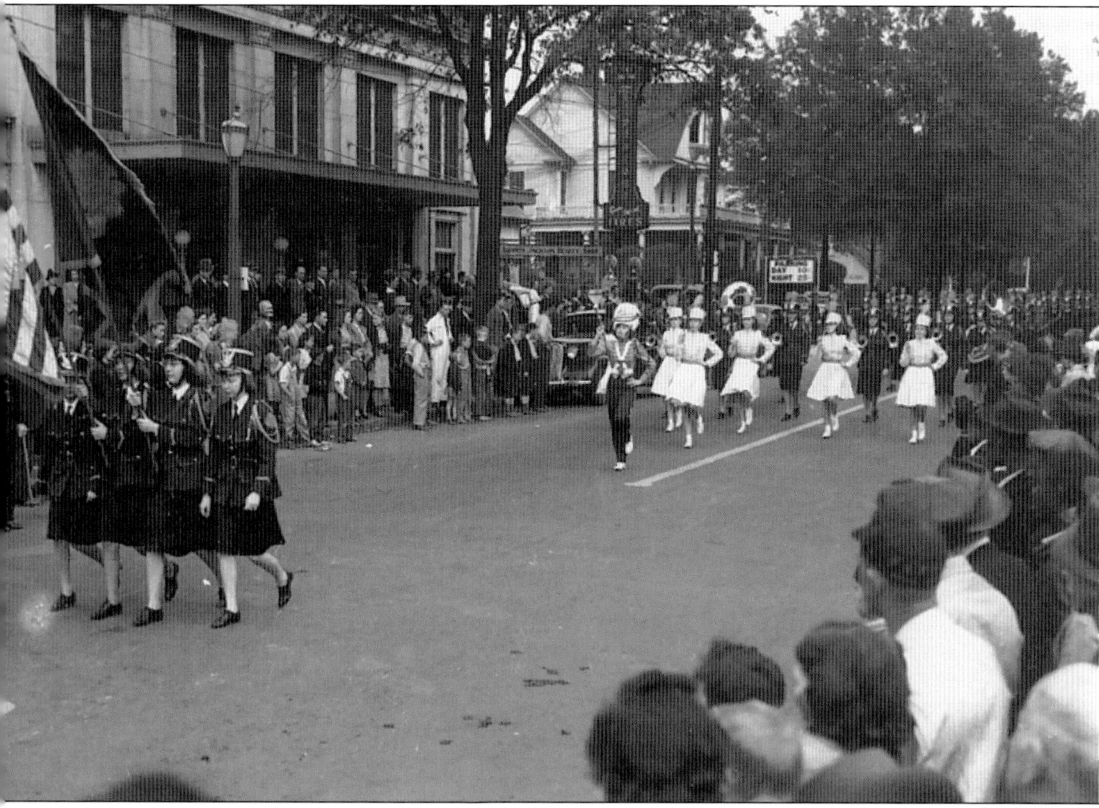

The entire town turned out for parades such as this one.

county fair would come, and Christmas parades, and at other times. I used to ride in all the parades. I had my own saddle horse back in the 1940s. There were three of us who had horses. You could keep them in your backyard. Back then, you could keep horses or cows, chickens, or anything in your backyard. Now, my father had a business. He had horses and he kept my horse over there in the stable.

"My father came here in 1909 from North Carolina. I was three months old in December of 1909. He came here to be with the Rock Hill Buggy Co. Then, it went into automobiles, so he was superintendent of the Anderson Motor Company.

"Then, you know, they went broke. Over on West Main, one time that was one of the main streets in Rock Hill, East Main and West Main. Our house was over there. There was a store there, a big store, and it was the old Captain A.D. Holler's store. Old Capt. and Mrs. Holler were the parents of old Mrs. John Gary Anderson, and our house was right next door to Capt... Everybody said "Captain." He was a captain in the War between the States. So, old Capt. Holler had this store. Well, when Anderson Motor Co. went broke, Daddy opened up old Capt. A.D. Holler's store, and it was two stores together. He made it into one. He had a grocery on one side and a market on the other. We didn't have chain stores then, and it was one of the leading stores in Rock Hill. Everybody knew Hall's Market and Grocery. Then you called up and had your groceries delivered.

"We had eight cotton mills operating in Rock Hill. You know, Rock Hill was a mill town. Well, I want you to know that Daddy, of course, had horses then. Well, he rigged up either two or three wagons. In the center was a

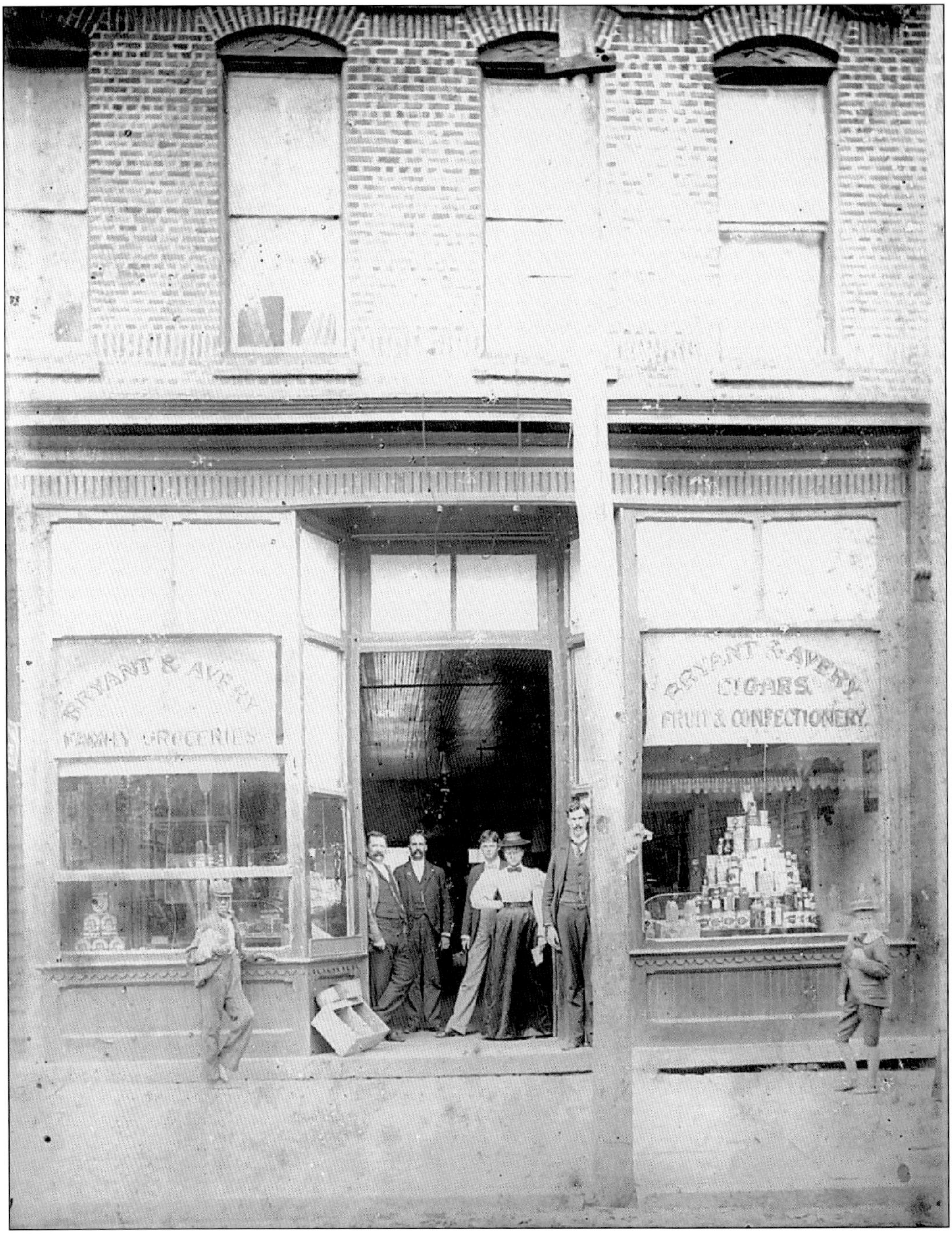

refrigeration place. These wagons would go out early in the morning, driven by horses, and they would work the cotton mills. The people would go out to the wagons and buy their groceries and their meat. They kept meat in the place that had the ice, you know...blocks of ice. And then they might come back in at lunch time, and restock. And I'm going to tell you something, the mill people were the ones that paid for their groceries. They ate, and they paid. It was the people on the other end of town, the people who were supposed to have the money, that were very slow in paying

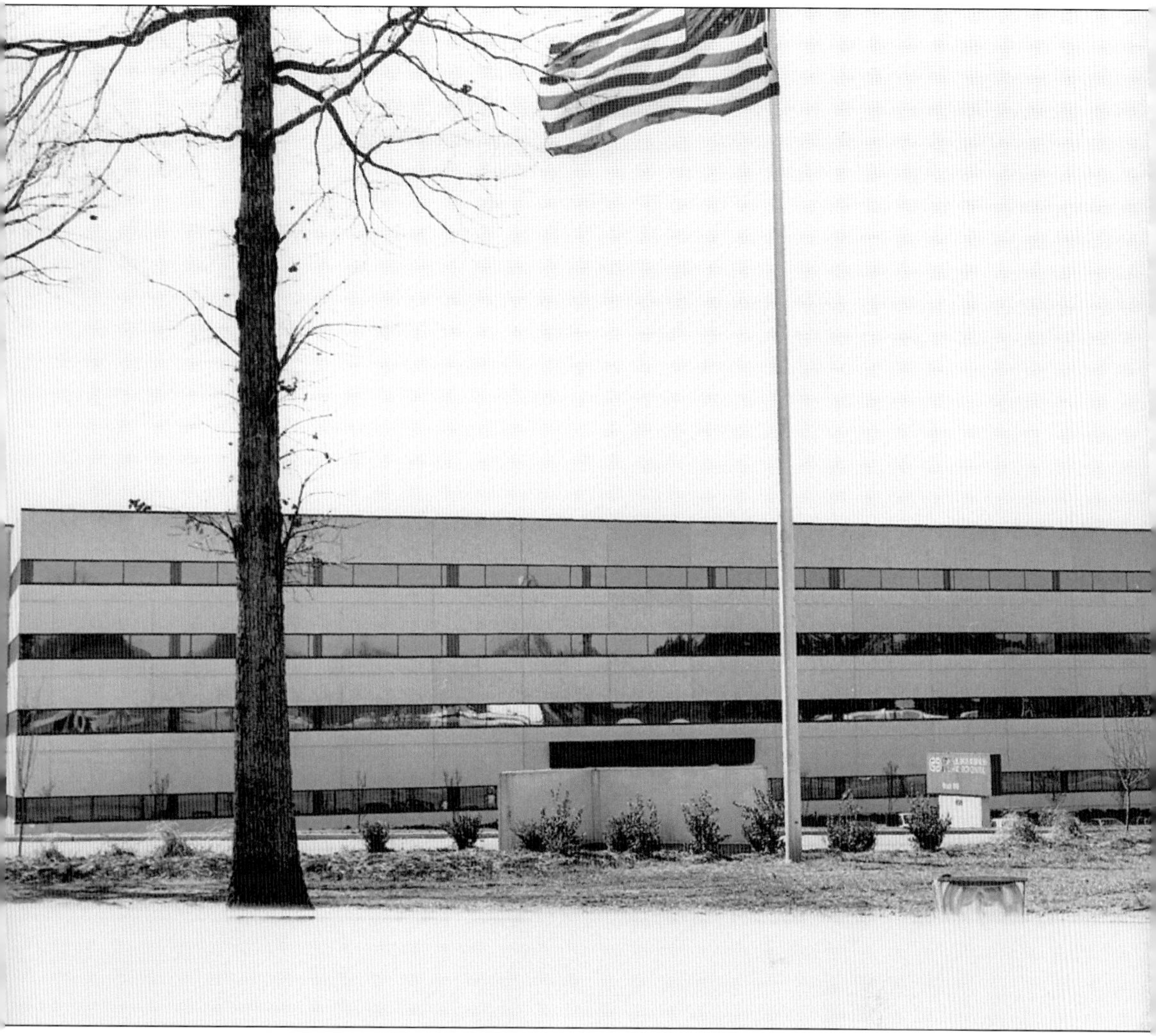

for their groceries. So Daddy was ahead of his time on account of rigging up these wagons and having them operate.

"Well, we lived on Main Street. The street went down a lot. The neighbors moved off, but Daddy never would leave because it was right near the store, and his health got bad, so he retired. He died in about 1937. It's been a long time ago. But Rock Hill has changed so much since then. You knew everyone. You knew all the skeletons in the families. But you know, in Rock Hill, there are quite a few skeletons around in the prominent families, so-called prominent families. I heard somebody's son who's very influential in politics in Rock Hill. The son said, 'I'm glad I can walk down Main Street, and people know who I am.' I thought, 'I'd like him to know some of the stuff I know about his family.' So you never know when it is safe to say something. I don't think it's as friendly as it once was. We have so many outsiders coming in. But it's a good town.

"I attended Winthrop Training School. Back then, we had a lot of plays; we had a lot of pantomime. I remember a big play we had up at Winthrop Training School. It was *Sleeping Beauty*. Believe it or not, I was Sleeping Beauty. And the strange part was that Margaret Mauldin, a girl, was the Prince. And I can see Margaret now. She was tall and thin and had a Prince uniform. She looked exactly like a boy. Then, one

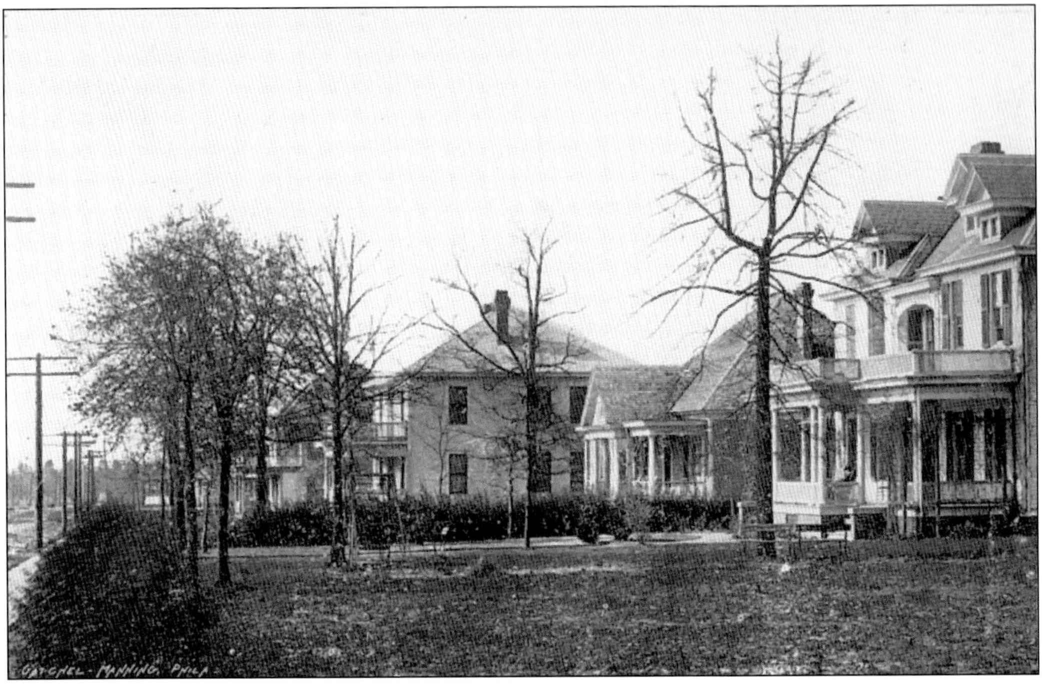

Woodland Park is pictured here in 1912.

time, we had a play down at Rock Hill High School, and I had a song dedicated to me. The music teachers wrote a song, "My Rose." I don't remember the tune, but I remember the words.

"I went to Training School. Then I changed to Rock Hill High School. Daddy let me change. He was all for Winthrop College, but he let me go to Rock Hill High School, and I'm glad I did because you got in with a different set of people, and it was better.

"Rock Hill High School was over on White Street. I could walk to school. And I walked up to Winthrop Training School. I remember in the winter time it would be so cold, and it seemed like we had a lot of snows. My mother would make us take a dry pair of socks. We'd have to change socks when we got to school.

"Back then we had one teacher. Winthrop girls taught during their senior year. That was good because it was a change, you know, and Winthrop Training School had a wonderful playground, slides and just a lot of playground equipment. I remember when we used to take lunch to school. I'm glad I lived back in the time I lived.

"We had a lunch box and Mama would make us a sandwich. You'd take a piece of cake or cookie. I can't remember anything about the drink. Another thing, we had a few people that went to Winthrop Training School that lived in Ebenezer, and they'd come in from Ebenezer, and they'd ride horseback, and they'd tie their horses out at the school and kept them there until school was out and then ride back home.

"My parents moved here in 1909. They had the maneuvers and had several old maids who got married during this time. And the town people really took them in. Now, in the big house over there I remember there was a shortage of places to stay, and I let some of them stay with us. My husband was living then.

"You know we had the WPA here at one time, and that was out in the Ebenezer section. The CCC camp was out where the water tower is.

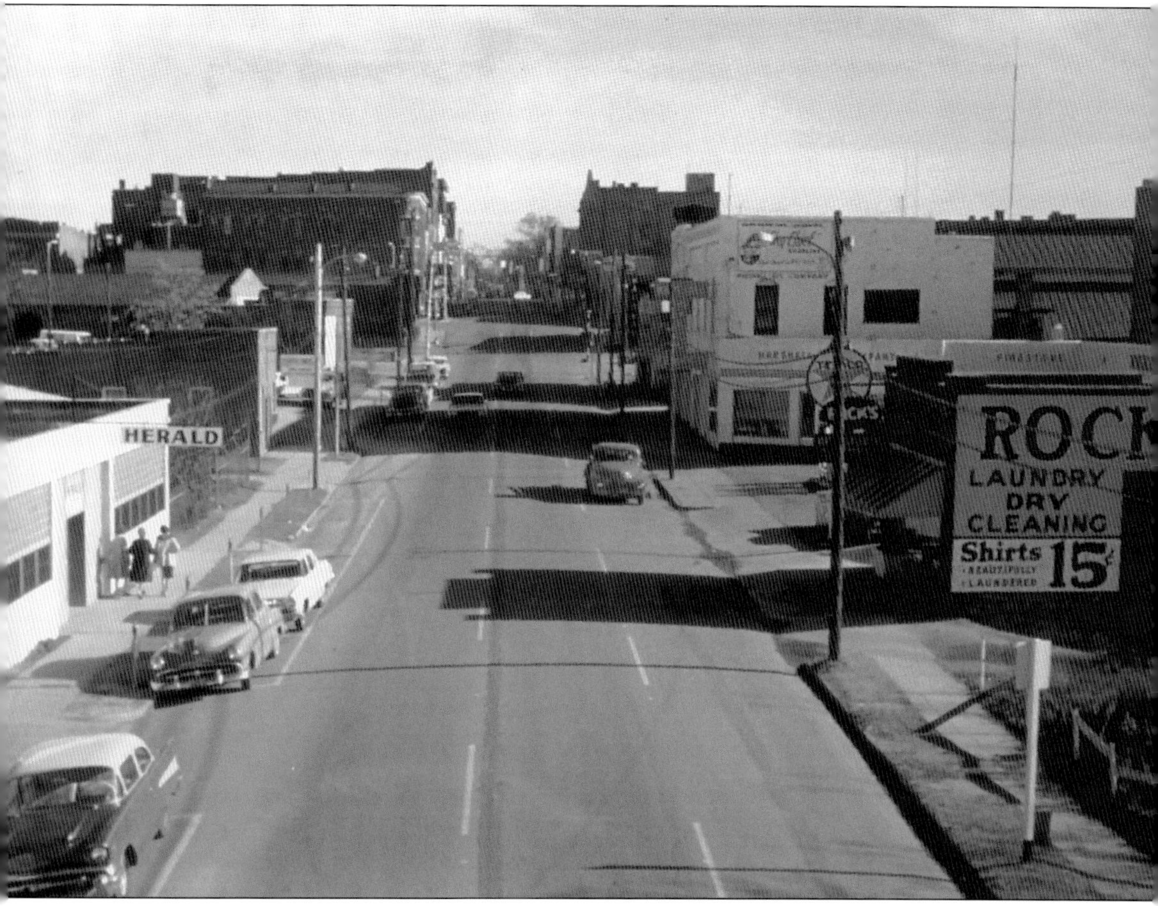

Shown here is Main Street looking east in the 1950s.

"Another thing. You'd go downtown. You'd go in a store and see something you liked and couldn't make up your mind. You could take it home on approval. You knew everybody back then.

"I remember Belk's. I remember Woolworth's, McCrorey's, and Friedham's. And when we were growing up, we couldn't buy any clothes except at Friedham's. Listen, you could buy a harness in there for your horse. At the back of the store they carried groceries, anything in farm equipment. You could buy anything in that store. And you knew the sales people. They wanted to sell. We had an Efird's on Main Street, too, and a Newberry's.

"The tornado of 1926 hit down in the black section, down on Crawford Road. It was bad. I remember how dark everything got. We didn't have any lights, and they called out the national guard that night. Another thing, my daddy liked dark Cornish hens, chickens. He raised them for show purposes, and he used to send them to Columbia and all around, and he won prizes. He won a silver trophy. I remember one time he won this beautiful mahogany rocking chair. We used to help him. When he'd get the chickens ready to ship to the fair, we'd help him polish them up and wash them and file those spurs. He wouldn't eat those white chickens we have now.

"I was raised in St. John's Methodist Church. We were Methodists. Then I married an ARP, and they were such

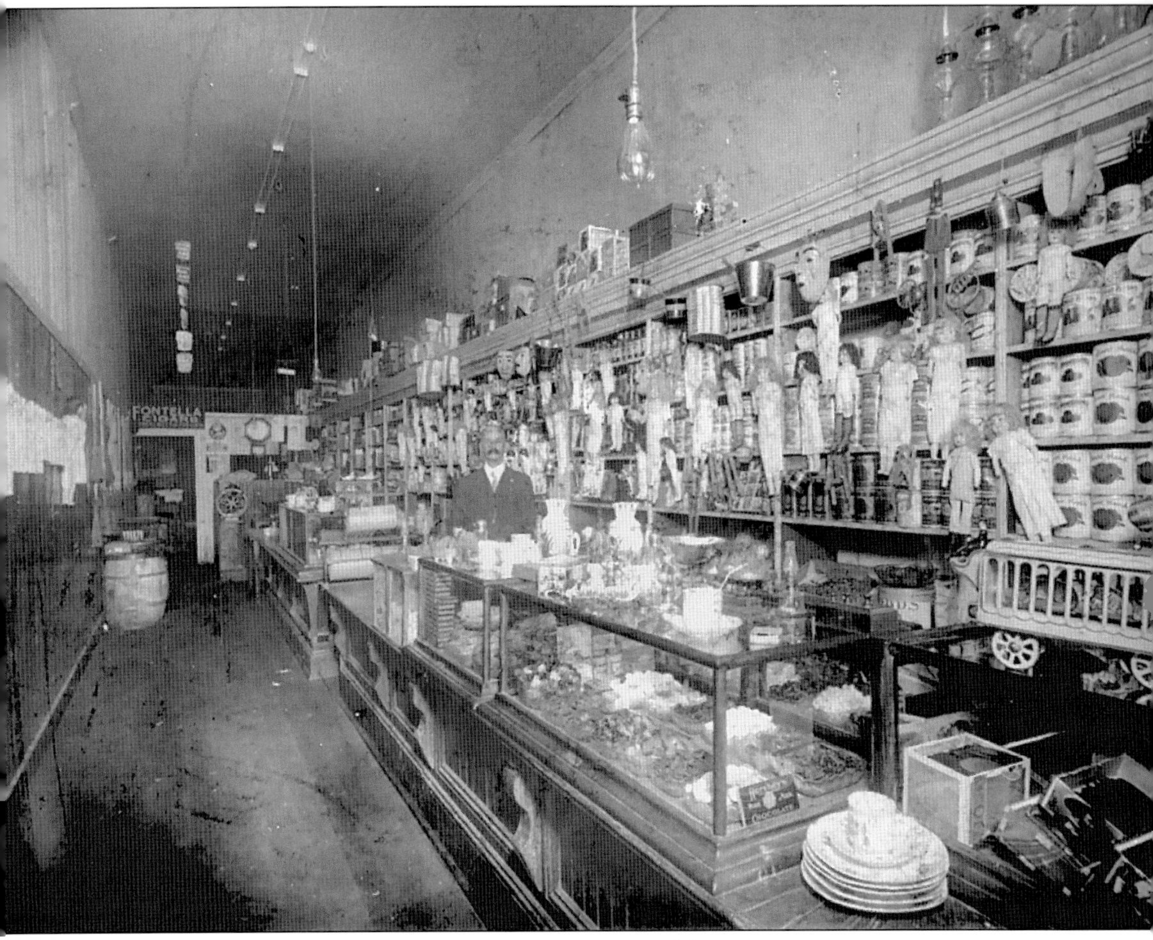

The inside of Bryant and Avery Grocery is pictured here, c. 1910.

dyed-in-the-wool ARP's that I joined that church. I've been in there for over 60 years.

"Everything was rationed during the war. You couldn't buy shoes and meat. We were lucky. Mr. Walter McKnight had a market down on Trade Street, and I remember we were able to get meat, or he would get extra ration coupons, and he'd let you have meat. We were able to get things, and the salesmen would bring silk hose. So we fared well, didn't have to do without anything. But it was bad, and so many of the Rock Hill boys had to leave for the war, and the Cowan boy was killed and the Walter Jenkins' son. We lost a few boys. And my sister was in the WAVES, and she ran into Johnny London overseas in the South Pacific during the war. So, you'd run up on somebody from home. It's a small world. I wish Rock Hill could go back to a quieter time.

"Things started changing after the war, and the mills closed down, and the Rock Hill Printing and Finish Co. saved Rock Hill. It saved Rock Hill because, see, Rock Hill was a mill town with eight cotton mills operating all the time, and then, when they stopped, it gave a long list of people in Rock Hill employment. There wasn't anything else here, and it meant a lot to them.

"We'd go up there to Charlotte for shopping. The merchants didn't like it, but we'd go up there and spend the day. In fact, it was an all-day trip. You wore your

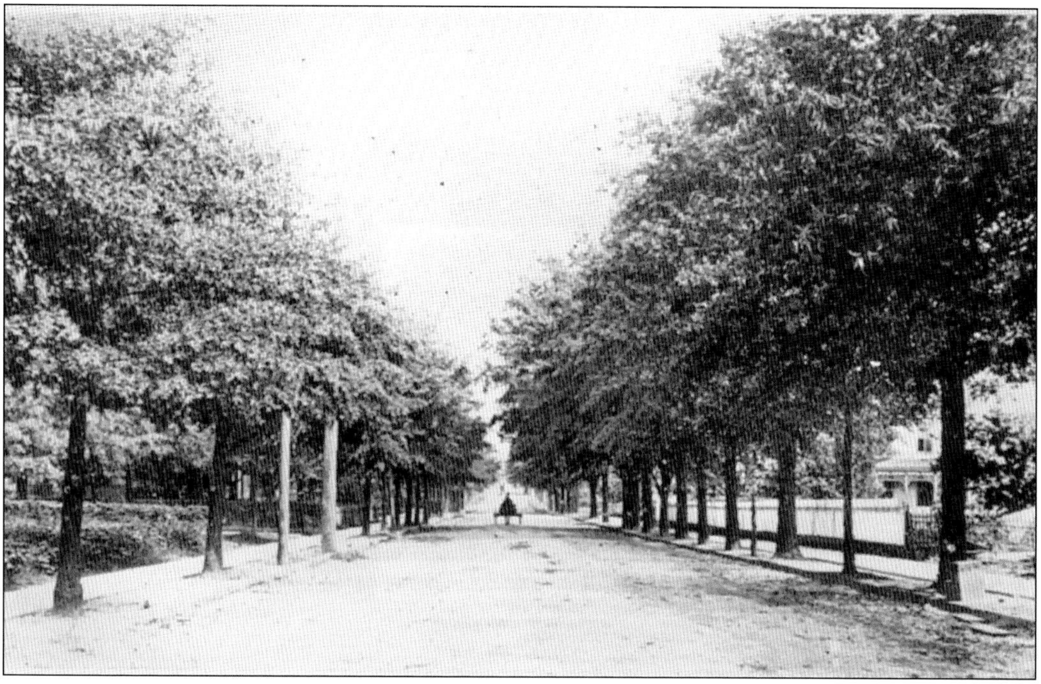

East Main Street is shown here in the early twentieth century.

hat. You wore your gloves, and you spent the day up there. About a year ago, I had someone call me and ask 'What can the merchants do to keep people shopping in Rock Hill?' I said, 'Listen, they've been trying to find the answer to that for 50 years, and they haven't found it yet!' Oh, I remember Friedham. He'd get mad if you'd go to Charlotte, and if you'd go in there to buy something, you'd better come out with something!

Old Rock Hill

Since Rock Hill is such a "New South" city, the phrase "Old Rock Hill" seems odd. After all, the village's population was only 100 persons in 1860. Ebenezer, which was gobbled up by an expanding Rock Hill in 1960, is a century older and was once larger. At the dawn of the present century, however, the population of Rock Hill was 6,000 citizens. Winthrop had found a new home here; by 1895, there were three cotton mills in operation, with two more under construction. Sharecroppers and tenant farmers, no longer able to earn a living on the land, flowed into town, bringing their energy and labor.

Therefore, "Old Rock Hill" does exist. It was built 100 years ago by the transplanted cotton mill workers and the textile magnates who accepted new economic realities. Barron and Clara Rawls Roddey represent the families who, in the early twentieth century, accumulated the

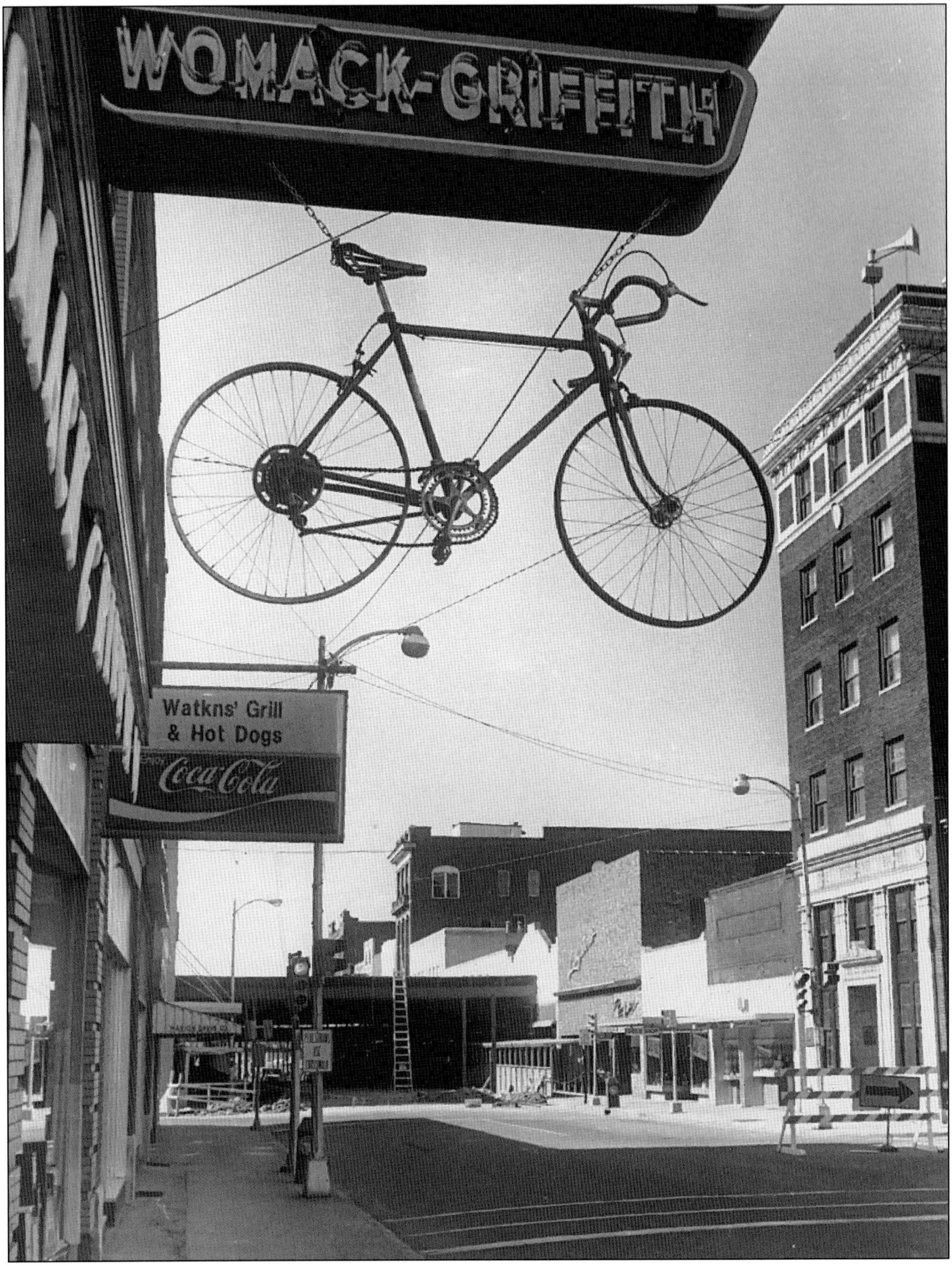

financial successes available in a growing New South city.

"Right across Oakland Avenue, where the Pix Theater is today, is where my grandfather Barron lived. He was John R. Barron. He built the Industrial Cotton Mill, which is still standing. In fact, he not only owned it, he built it on the farm. He made the brick right there.

"Our house, the one in which I grew up, is right across the street. It's still standing, right beside the Pix Theater.

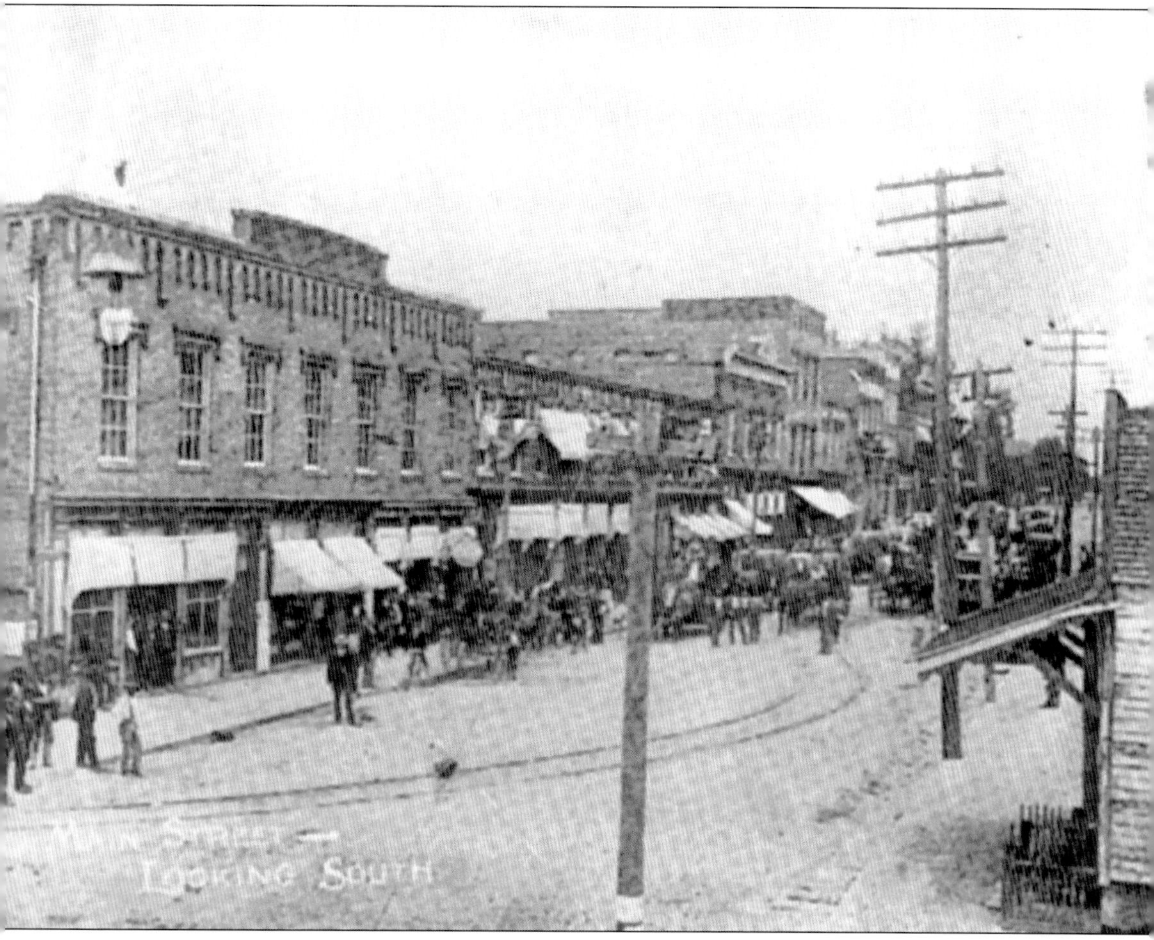

Here is an 1895 view of Main Street looking south.

"My family owned the Victoria Cotton Mills, and it was one of the first, if not the first, to run on electricity. Most of the mills were built on the river.

"As a young man, we had a pool table on the third floor. The boys called it "Roddey's pool hall." Oh, I was very popular! As you came in the front door, there was this monstrous hall. To the left was what we called the library. To the right there was a smaller room called the Japanese room and behind that the den. From the den was my grandmother's greenhouse, on the porch. And there was one bedroom downstairs. There was a kitchen and a dining room. Oh, with a very large table, beautiful chandelier. I thought the most striking feature was the spiral staircase. The hall was so huge, they had a three piece orchestra play for the dances. That's where they had their parties in the big central hall. The house was built in 1912. I know my grandfather told my dad that he had to give the man additional money to complete it. As you walked in, the woodwork was solid mahogany, and it cost $47,000. Can you believe that?

"We had quite a few mills. Rock Hill Printing and Finishing Co. was about the biggest, but then there was the Industrial Mill, which my grandfather Barron started. And there was the old Victoria Mill, which was the Roddey Mill. Both grandfathers were into textiles. And then there was the Aragon right below the Industrial. And then that old mill that is still standing

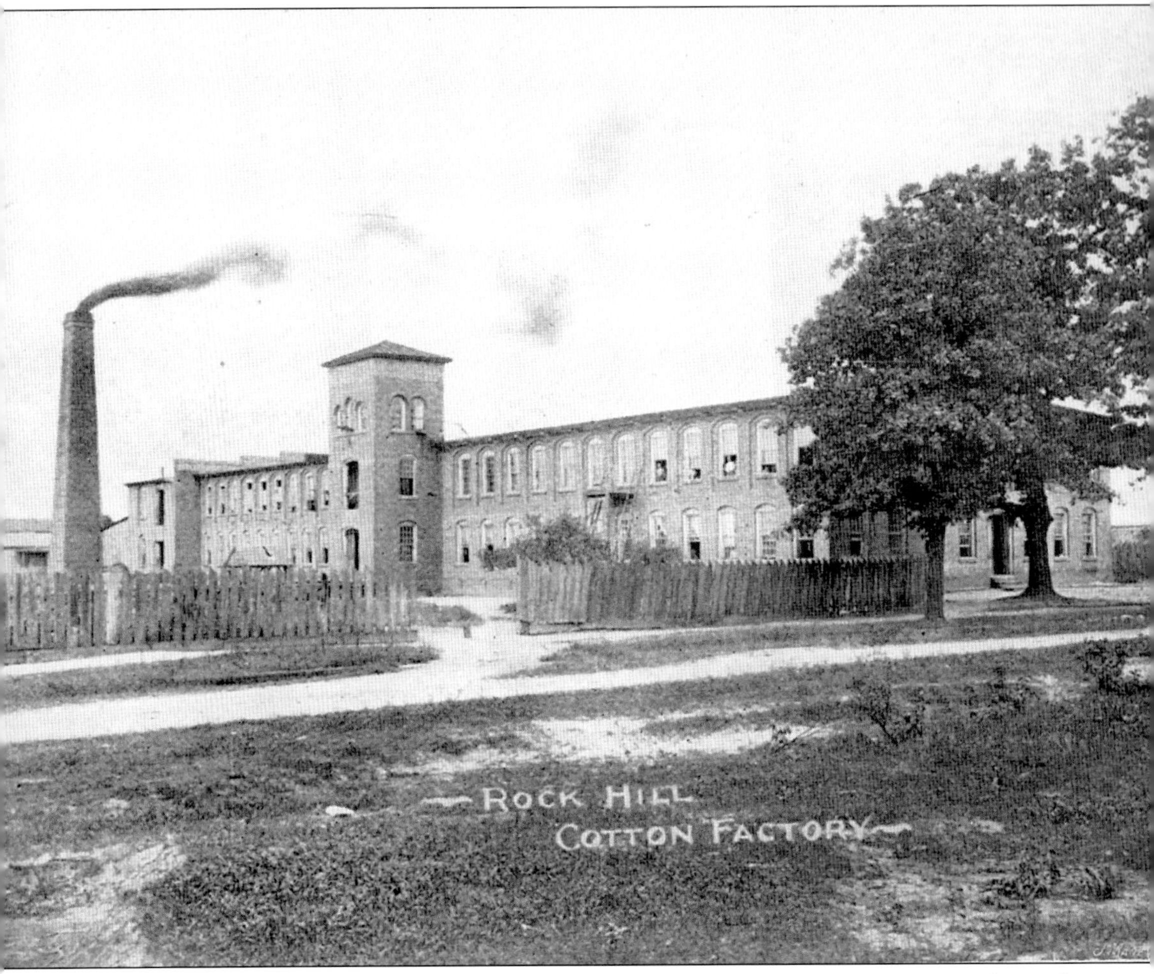

there, Plej's? That was the old Republic, I believe they called it. I think it changed hands three or four times.

"And I want to tell you about President and Mrs. Taft. You know they came to Winthrop. They spent the night at the Roddey home. The house was fairly new then. Papa Joe, my grandfather, was a trustee at Winthrop longer than anybody else had ever been. I forget how many years he was a trustee. I believe, in one article I read, it said he had been a trustee from the beginning until his death. You know his portrait is in the Dunlap-Roddey room.

"They didn't have any secret service when the Tafts came to visit. Upstairs, there was kind of an apartment, 'Suite,' I think they called it. Two bedrooms and bath. I don't know. I heard they had to get a special size tub for the president. Those old tubs were big anyhow, you know.

"They had a dust chute from the second floor down to the basement. In other words, with sweeping and whatever, you didn't have to carry it. You just swept it in this chute, and it went to the basement. Somehow a spark got in there and started a fire. It didn't do a whole lot of damage outside of smoke damage.

"I can remember where you go down at the end of Main Street, coming up on the right there was a little hotel there. Right there, well it used to be Ratterree's Drug Store. Above it was a photographer. Thackston's it was called. Then there was the Andrew Jackson hotel.

"I remember the dining room at my grandparents' home had two sideboards.

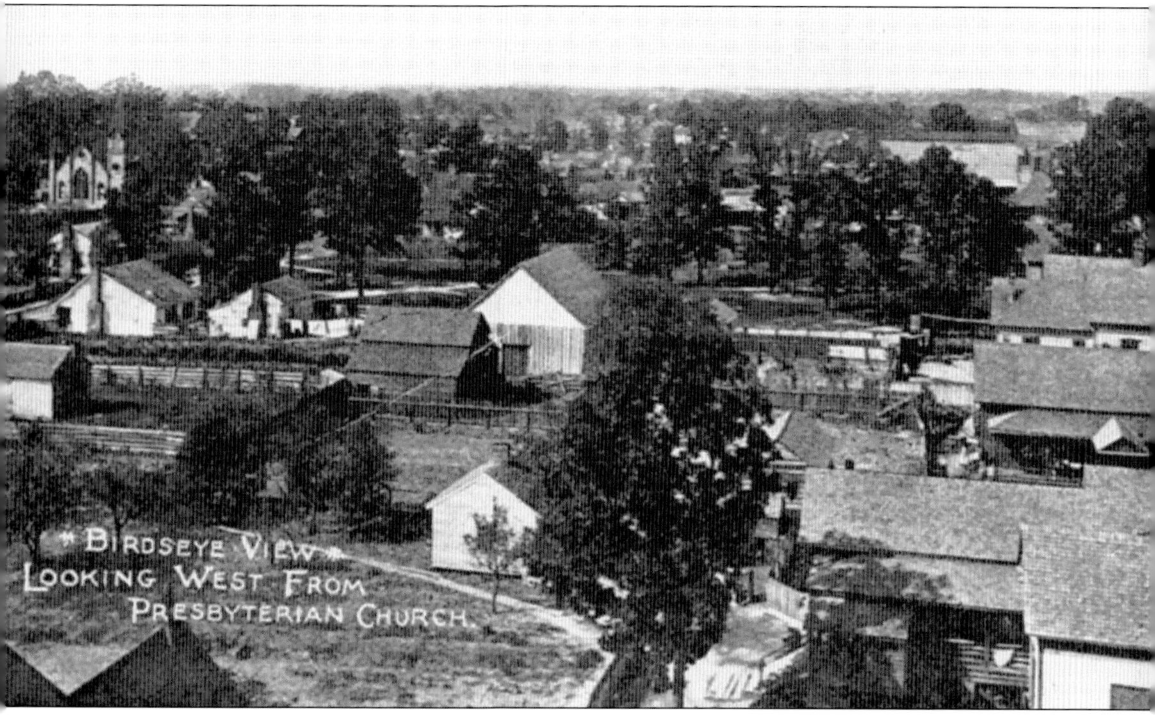

We had electric buttons to summon the servants. And I think Mama Jo had four. She, Mama Jo, had a nurse, a housekeeper, a cook, a yard man, and a chauffeur. Well, it was the finest home that's ever been built in Rock Hill. It had a vacuum cleaning outlet in each room.

"Everybody gathered at the Good shop. That was the little shop across from Winthrop. The building is still there beside Withers building.

"There were two movie theaters downtown. You know, in the summer time, we had a swimming pool, and we'd go and dance at a pavilion beside it. We had house parties.

"The Roddey House was a landmark in Rock Hill. I watched 'em trying to tear it down. They had a devil of a time doing it. We have some of the crystal doorknobs. There was a copper light fixture that was over the pool table and a chandelier, alabaster.

"A screech owl somehow got in Oakland Avenue Church. . .right up over the choir loft, and they tried every way in the world to get the dern owl out of there. So somebody mentioned it to Daddy, so Daddy just went up there and shot him. They say he just fell flat. Daddy was a sure shot. But the funny thing now is we just had a reunion at our church. They honored all the members who had been members for 50 years. So Barron was one of those members. You had to tell any stories you remember. Barron told that one, but, you know, now, that didn't go over. You don't shoot a bird...especially in church!"

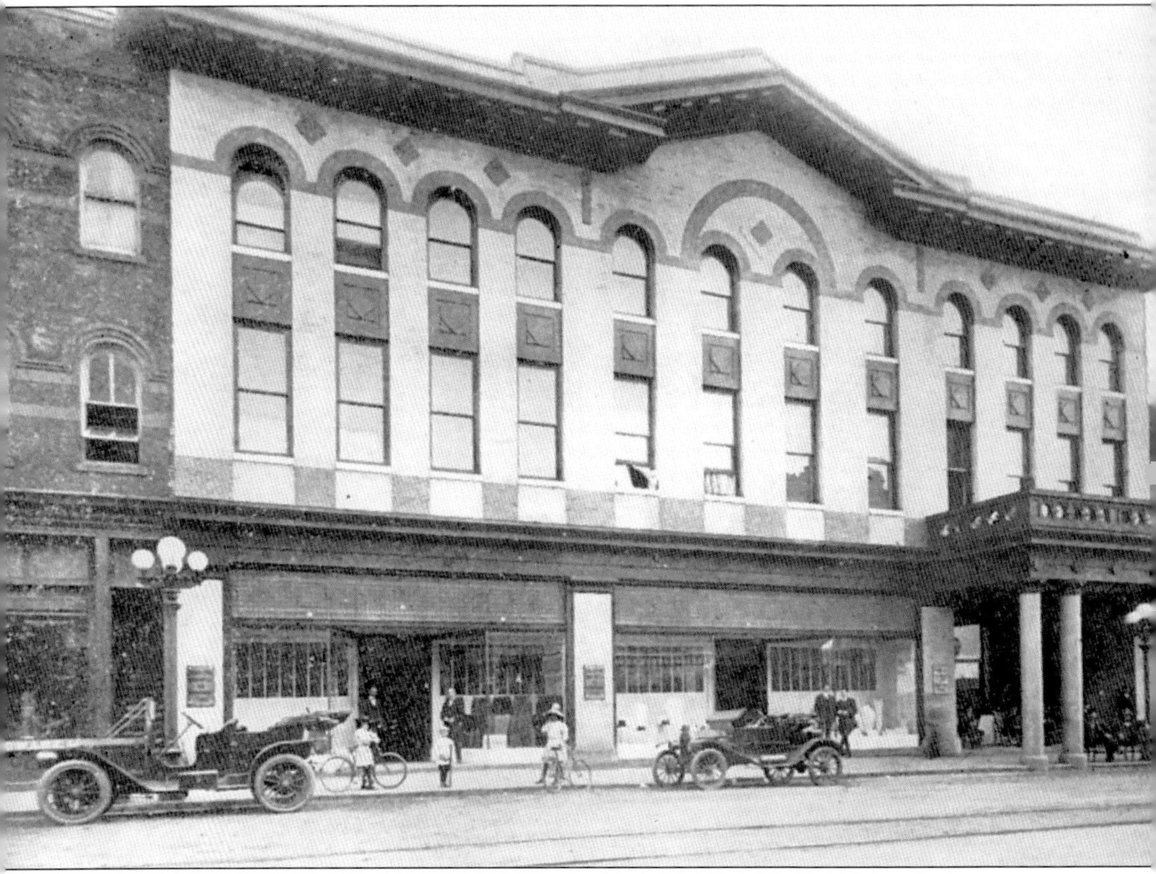

One of Old Rock Hill's most popular meeting locations was the Carolina Hotel.

MADE IN DIXIE

New South cities such as Rock Hill produce entrepreneurs who are willing, in a 1990s phrase, "to think outside the box." Realizing that buggies were rapidly being eclipsed by automobiles as the twentieth century's preferred mode of transportation, John Gary Anderson began producing cars in Rock Hill in 1915. While his goal was to make Rock Hill a southern Detroit, he ultimately failed to grasp the market demands for cheap, assembly line–produced automobiles. Thus, his innovative plans for a luxury line of painstakingly built cars ended in financial disaster for his company in 1926.

Here, Dr. Edward Lee recalls "Mr. Anderson's Automobile" in its heyday. At the wheel was a bold businessman with an aggressive advertising strategy to showcase cars "made in Dixie."

"Six cars were designed, built, and tested in 1915. In January 1916, Anderson held a grand reception at Rock Hill's Carolina Hotel to unveil his Anderson 6-40-6 before a crowd that included South Carolina Governor Richard Irving Manning, James J. Parian of the Curtis Publishing Co., and W.W. Ball, editor of *The State* newspaper of Columbia.

"To soft music and light refreshments, local residents and prospective buyers inspected the Anderson auto, which, for dramatic effect, was bathed in electric light. Over 1,000 people attended the

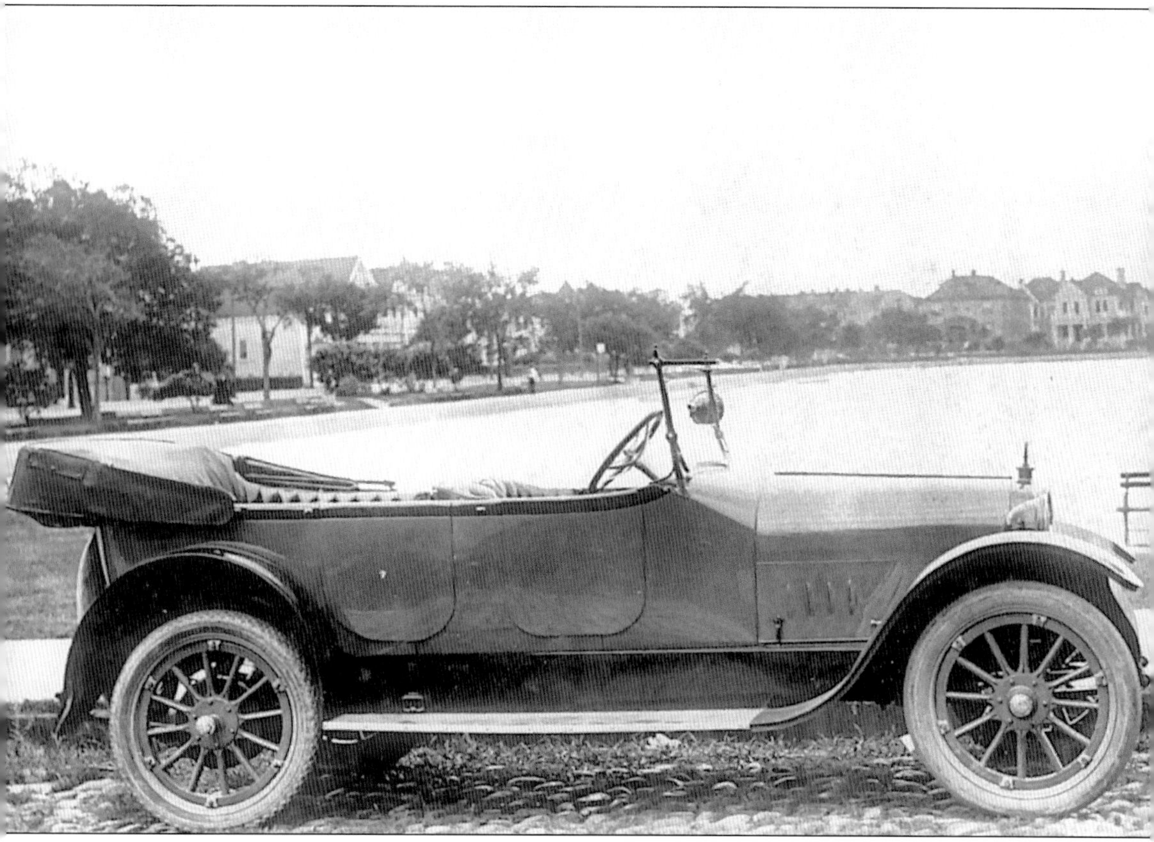

In 1920, an Anderson Car graced Charleston's Colonial Lake.

showing—an exciting beginning for the aspiring entrepreneur.

"The features of the Anderson 6-40-6 included 12-spoke wheels made of the best South Carolina hickory; Westinghouse electrical equipment, including a trouble lamp with cord and a cigar lighter; 33-inch by 4-inch oversize tires; and a six-cylinder engine capable of delivering 38 actual horsepower at 200 rpm.

"The car had two standard bodies—a three-passenger roadster and a four-passenger touring car—both painted Brewster green with black fenders and hoods. Other color combinations were optional. A heater and rumble seat for the roadster were available. The automobile also had a ventilating windshield, a 60-mile-per-hour speedometer, luggage straps on one running board, an engine-driven tire pump with gauge and hose, a spotlight mounted on the windshield post on the driver's side, and a full set of tools, including jack and wrench.

"Anderson announced that his motor company would be capitalized at $1.5 million. There would be 150,000 shares with a par value of $10 a share. Half of the issue would be common stock and the other half 7 percent preferred. The company's letterhead listed John Gary as president and his son, J.W., as manager.

"By 1917 Anderson's company had orders for all the cars it could produce—an estimated 1,100. This meant $1 million in sales and a payroll of $100,000. These figures were provided in an Anderson company advertisement that predicted the enterprise would be a great success. The ad's message was strong:

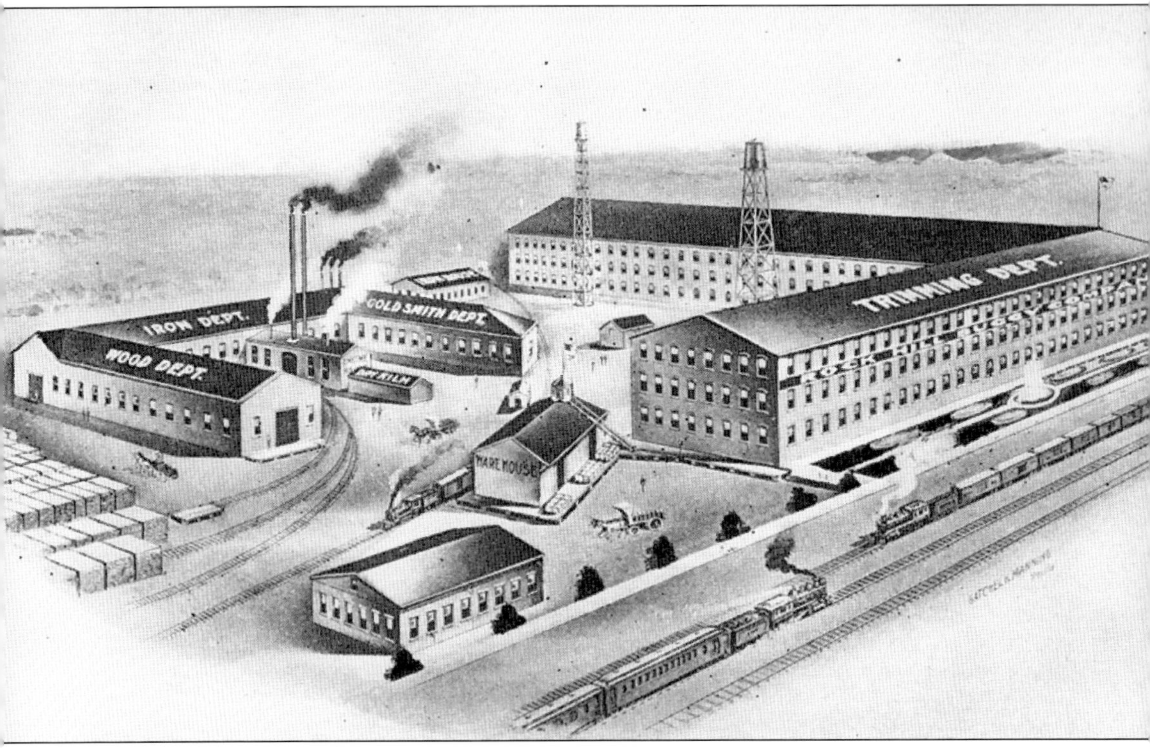

The birthplace of the Anderson Car was the Rock Hill Buggy Factory.

'Some of the Detroit factories making a car not over $1,000 paid dividends this year of nearly 200 percent. These factories are turning out five thousand cars per annum. Why can't this be done in the South—even in Rock Hill? It can and we believe it will. You have an opportunity of getting in on the ground floor. Will you do it, or will you hold back and let the 'other fellow' get in, and then in a year or two moan your ill luck? You can't possibly lose anything—because the business is going to be conservatively and efficiently managed—but you have the chance of making a small fortune. Will you take it?"

"Although the entry of the United States into World War I threatened to stunt the company's growth, Anderson made the best of the wartime situation by securing government contracts with the aid of Sen. Benjamin Tillman to construct small trucks and trailers. In his autobiography, Anderson mentions that the company had secured contracts for 3,000 small trucks, but only about 100 were assembled and shipped by the firm because the war ended quickly. The company also produced a number of trailer-type vehicles for hauling aircraft. Anderson gained valuable manufacturing experience during the war and made a healthy profit as well.

"The Anderson Motor Company's future looked so promising that, between 1918 and 1919, its board of directors voted twice to increase the company's stock. During the first few years after the war, the company's growth reflected that enjoyed by the American automobile industry, which was experiencing a tremendous boom. Stocks rose sharply, manufacturers could not keep up with demand, and dealers could sell at any price.

"Company sales rose sharply. Its best year financially was 1920, when a total of 1,180 units were built. Anderson employed about 200 workers who, to keep up with demand, were making autos as fast as they could.

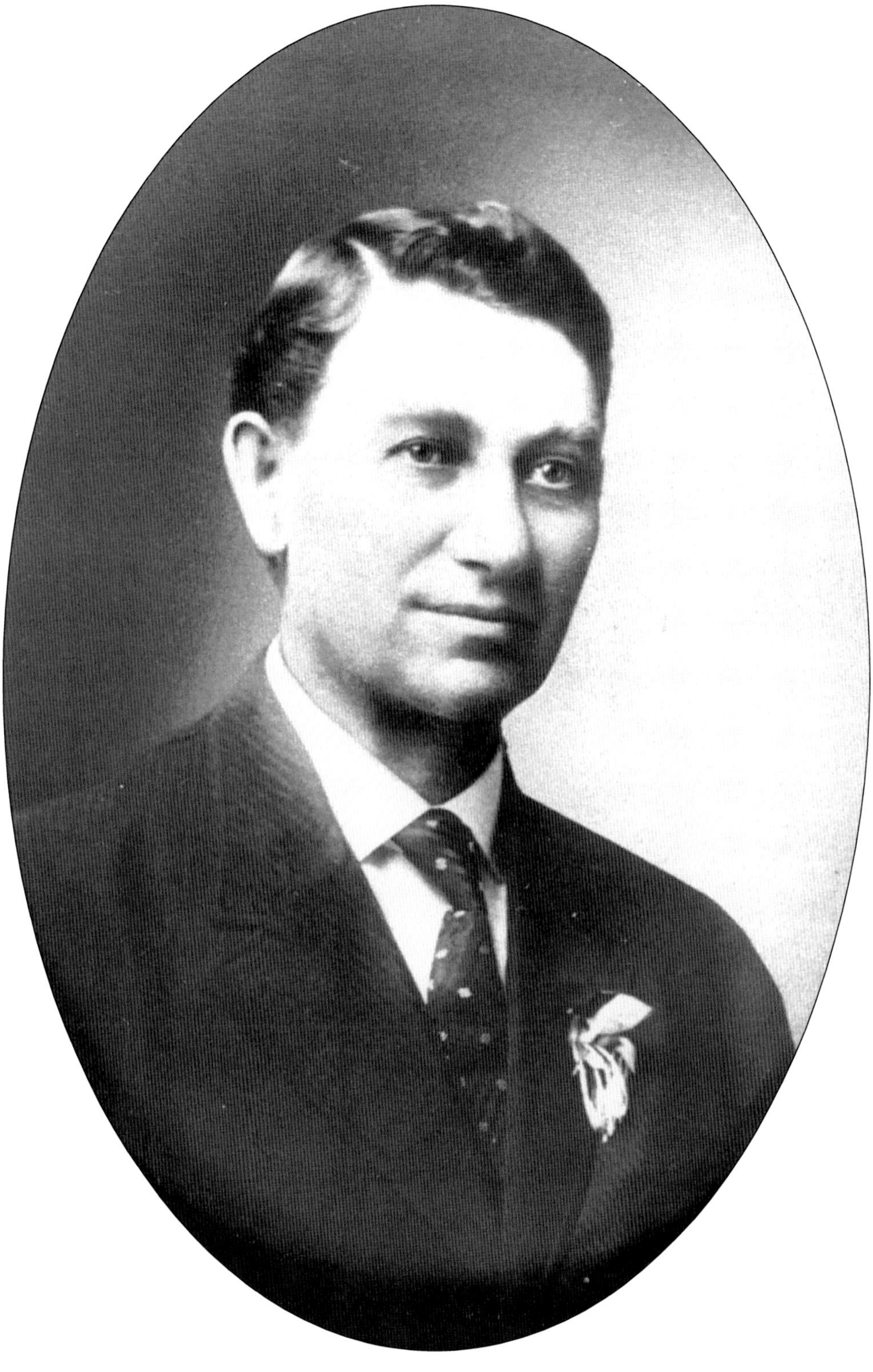

John Gary Anderson is pictured here in 1898 at age 37.

VISITORS WELCOME

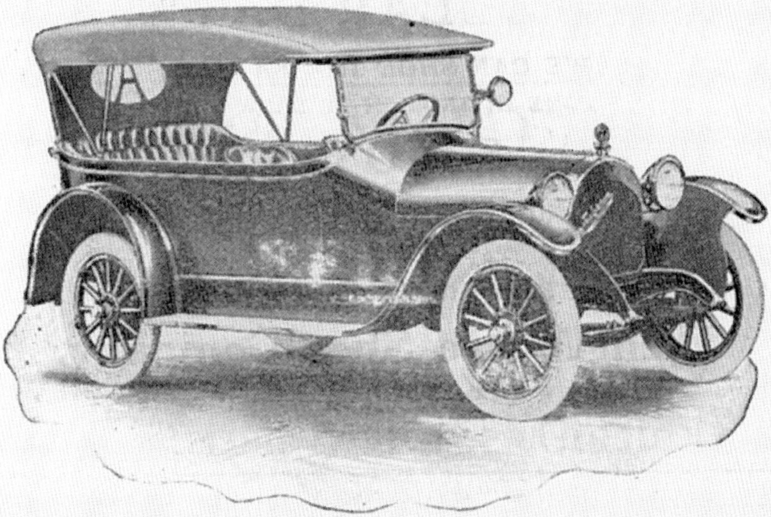

FOR INFORMATION WRITE

"A LITTLE HIGHER IN PRICE, BUT"

ANDERSON

SIX-40

ROCK HILL, S.C.

ANDERSON MOTOR CO.

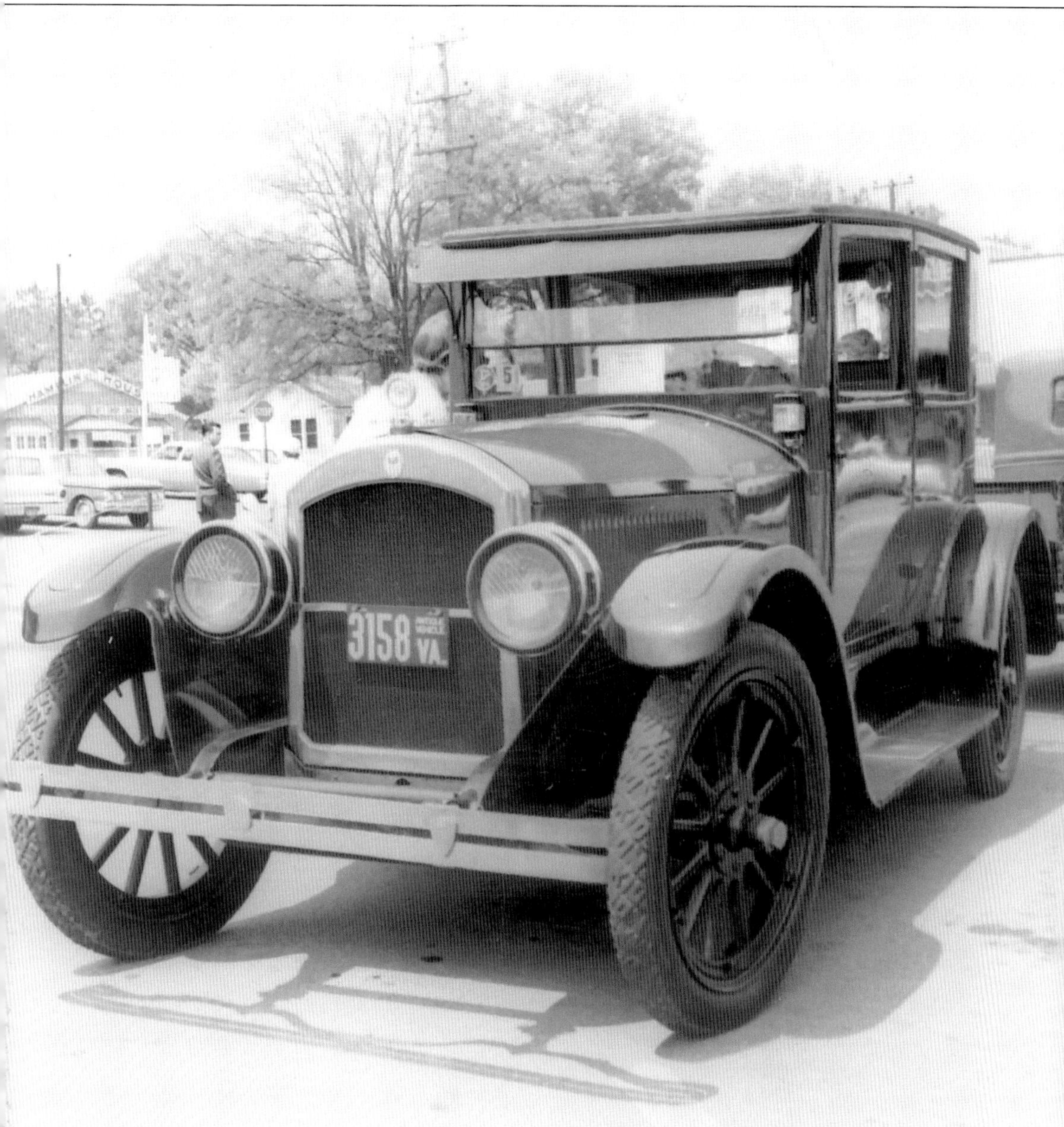

A 1919 Anderson car is pictured here.

"The year 1920 also saw major developments in types of cars made by Anderson's company. Anderson announced a convertible three-seater, which was adapted from the standard five-passenger touring body by attaching a special curved metal section across the back seat. The company also began making a six-passenger convertible that became known as the Convertible Six and sold for $1,675. The model could be transformed into either a roadster or a touring car. By 1921, company prices ranged from $1,650 for the five-passenger touring car to $2,550 for the sedan.

"By the early 1920s, the company had established an organization of 150 dealers, with a large commission house in New York City handling sales in foreign countries. The company's physical plant expanded, adding two buildings and occupying two acres. With production reaching 500 cars per month, Anderson advertised for more and more workers.

"Challenging Henry Ford, Anderson publicly boasted that more of his cars were sold in the heart of that auto manufacturer's country, Detroit, than in South Carolina, where 3,000 stockholders resided. The price for an Anderson was much higher than a Ford, which could be bought for prices ranging between $345 and $760. In an attempt to increase his business locally, Anderson used the advertising slogan 'A Little Bit Higher in Price, but—Made in Dixie.'

Home Brew

Even Rock Hillians who move to other places have lasting memories of our town. Joe Moore of Manning, South Carolina, grew up on Marion Street. In this interview, he shares a few recollections about radio, a Studebaker, a modest Winthrop student, and home brew.

"My father, Francis Heyward Moore (Hey), and Ida Huey Moore built our home. All five children were born here: Francis Heyward Jr., Elizabeth Moore Sykes, Jimmie Moore, Joe D. Moore, and Marion Moore.

"I remember a tornado struck in 1926 and knocked the top of our chimney through the roof and living room floor. I must have been about 12 years old.

"Dr. Simpson, who lived on the corner, had the first radio that I had ever seen. There were some 20 or 30 men and boys on his front porch to listen to John M. Lewis fight someone in London.

"Mr. Walter Brice had the first Frigidaire and had the agency to sell same. The rest of us got ice from a horse-drawn wagon that made daily deliveries.

"I can't remember our telephone number but do remember Huey Chevrolet was 757. Now it takes a college graduate to dial long distance.

"I remember when we got a Heatrola that would heat most of the house. A big improvement over fireplaces.

"My father bought a Studebaker car with isonglass windows. He couldn't drive, but mother thought she could, backed out of the backyard and knocked the corner off the porch. Six men from Rock Hill were on jury duty in York and took turns using their cars. Two of the men were excused and the other four got through court 10 at night, and none could drive. Walking down the street in York, they asked three or four men if they could drive and turn the car around and head same to Rock Hill. None

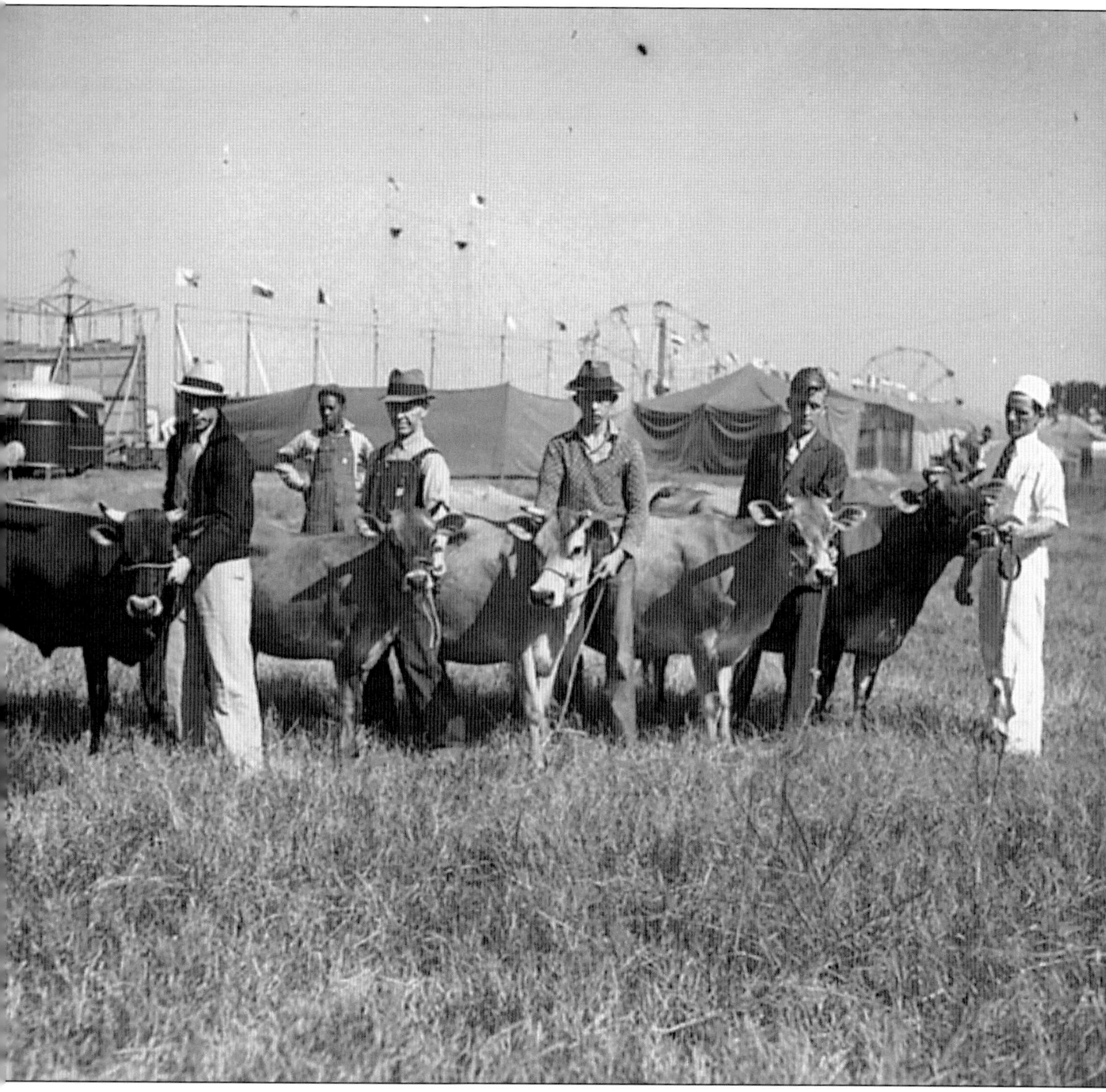

These prize cows were displayed at the York County Fair in the 1930s.

could drive, and all said a fellow that could drive was in the Pool Room. They found the fellow, and he headed the car out and jumped off the running board. They got in the ruts and made it home.

"I have so many fond memories of growing up in Rock Hill, but two things come to mind that I still laugh at when I think of them. First, all Winthrop girls wore uniforms, blue long dresses. My father had a shoe store and was fitting a Winthrop girl in shoes. He was facing the girl sitting on a stool, and she was looking in a mirror and looked up and threw her dress over my father's head. My father was bald headed, and she thought it was her knee cap!

"Our house was bricked up on the front and the back was some 5 feet off the ground. I must have been eight years old and playing in the backyard when I saw someone run and hide behind a brick pillar. I thought they were robbers and threw a rock and told them to come out. I heard laughing and recognized John S.

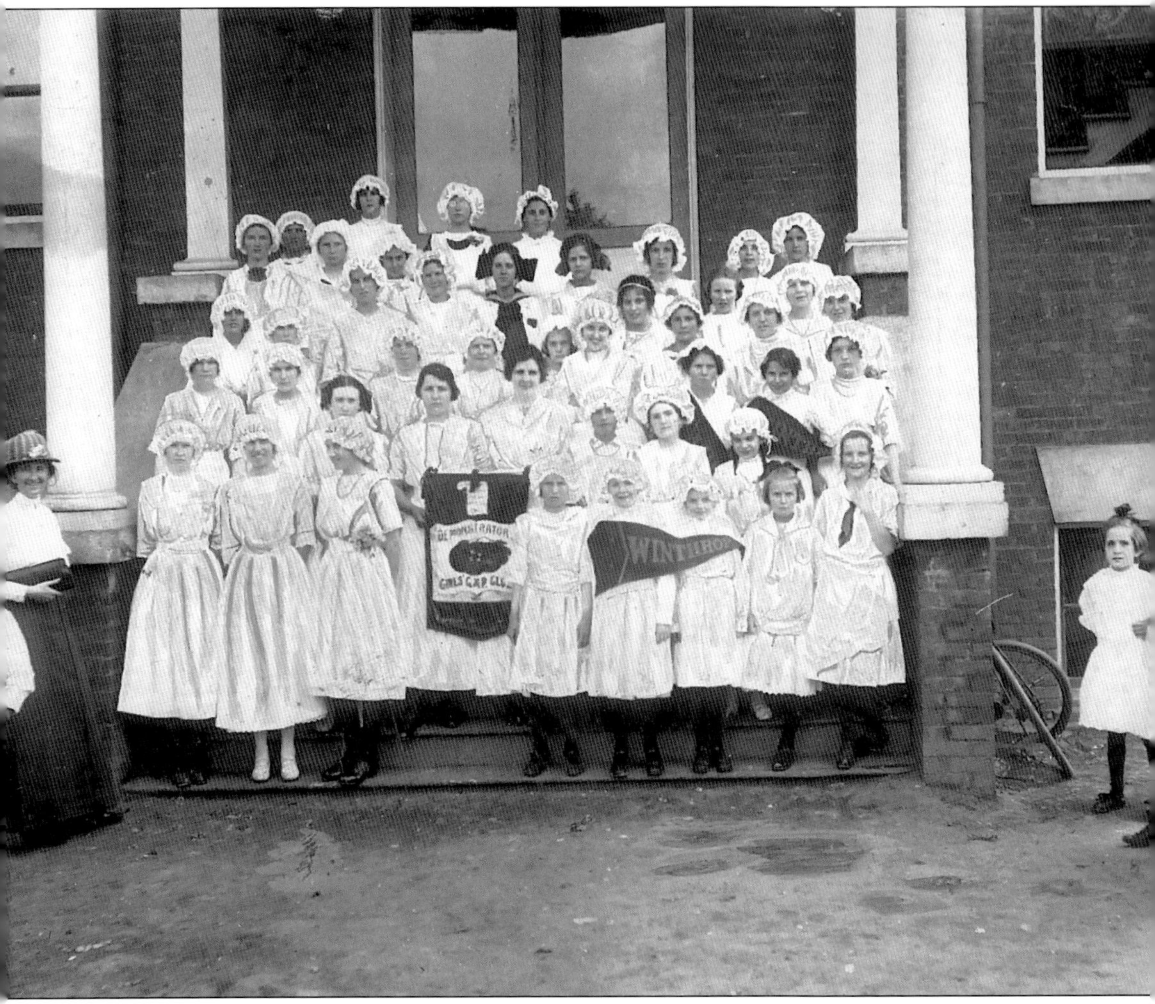

Women and girls gather in 1914 for a meeting of the Tomato Club.

Goodman. Heyward, my oldest brother, and others were making home brew under our house (this was during prohibition). I went under there and was told that I could eat all the raisins I wanted, if I wouldn't tell Mother or Daddy. They had quite a set up: sugar, raisins, big glass containers that Springs Mill used to get dye in from Germany, and a big barrel, bottles, caps. When Mother came home and I told her, she could hardly get her breath. When Daddy came home and was told all H broke loose. He told them to pour all of it out down the street drain. Jack Anderson, a jeweler, lived four houses down from our house, told them not to pour it out but to put it in his garage. Jack had two little boys, Jack and Doodle. After some three days, it was decided the brew should be ready to bottle. The brew was in a big wooden barrel with cheese cloth over same. John S. Goodman put a hose in the barrel and sucked up a good swig. Jack and Doodle both started laughing and finally admitted they had been using same for the bathroom. That put an end to making home brew.

"Recently, while in Rock Hill, I drove down Marion Street and can't understand how the hill isn't as steep and the homes are closer to the street than they used to be."

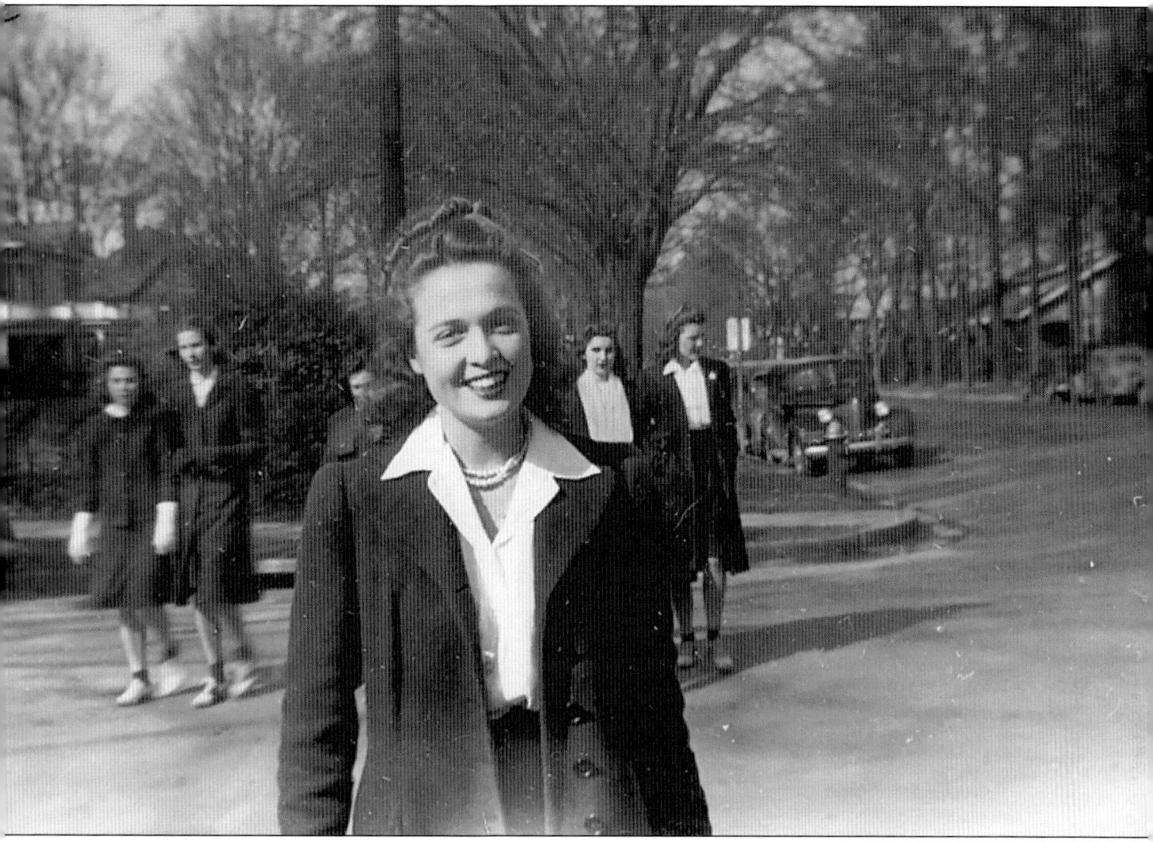

In the early 1940s, these women took an autumn walk.

First Class

Looking back on his life, Jimmy Rhea, a realtor, has a sense of satisfaction that his hometown has become "first class." In the following interview, Mr. Rhea reminisces about a destructive fire, his World War II service, luring companies to Rock Hill, and the hard work which produced a "first class city."

"When I was a little boy of about four years of age, there was a stable for horses and mules. It was located on East Black Street about where the York County Library is today. Between where the library and the police station is now. Anyway, the livery stable caught fire in the middle of the night. Twenty or twenty-five horses and mules burned up in the fire. The fire's flames woke me up. We lived there on the corner, across from where city hall is today, and after I awoke, I went downstairs. It was so intense of a fire that I put my nose against our window, and you could feel the heat. And I was half a block away from the stable! That was in the 1920s sometime.

"As World War II started for us, I went down on a train to Columbia to report to Fort Jackson. There were five people who rode down together. Three of us came back home. Two of our group were killed in the Normandy invasion. You feel fortunate to get back home. I was in the service for three years. So many of our people lost their lives. You know how powerful the United States is today. None of that could have happened without the sacrifices of the soldiers and those people back home.

"We have become a first class city. Not just in size, but in amenities. Way back, it wasn't a very big place. Our success

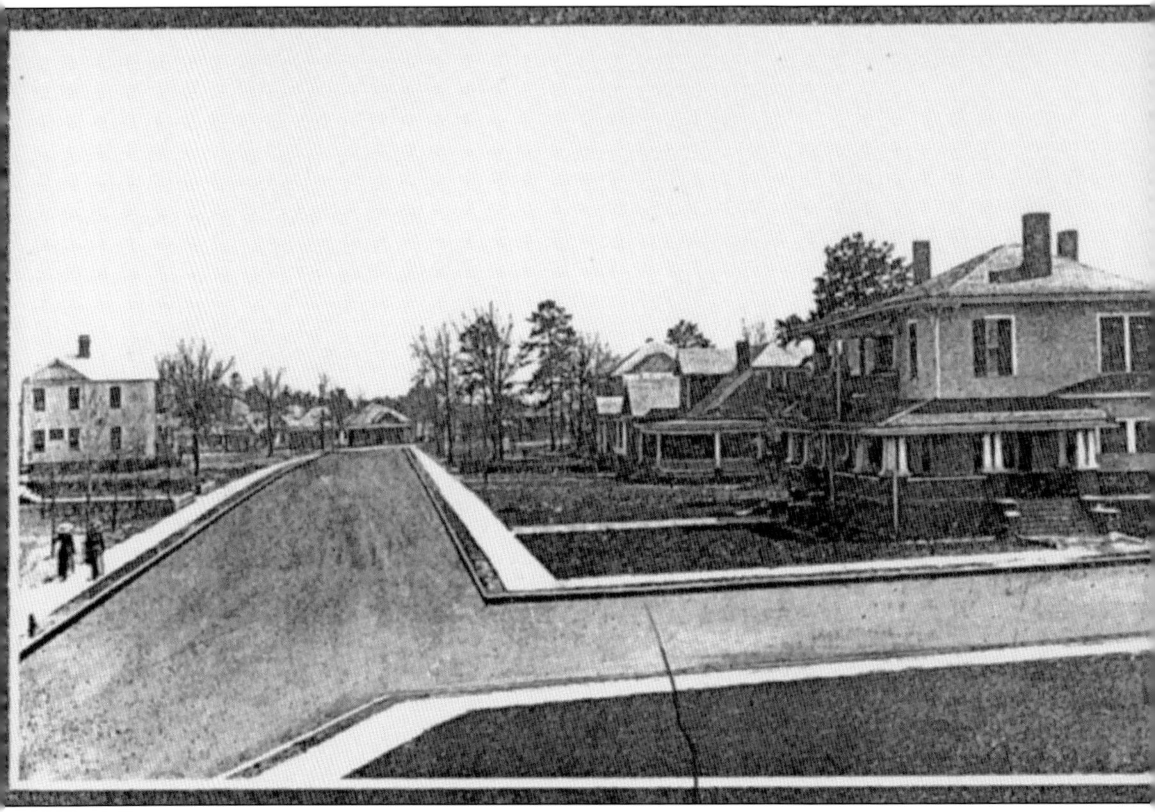

Marion Street is pictured here in the 1920s.

is due to the fact that we've had good leadership over the years. People really cared about the city. They wanted to do well.

"I can remember back in the 1970s. I was on the South Carolina State Development Board. Now, it's called the Commerce Department. I represented this district, district 16, on the board. Back then, I can remember, as far as industry was concerned, I was always on the executive director to bring industrial prospects to Rock Hill. They would take them to Columbia instead. Then to Greenville and Charleston. And we were kind of the last ones on the list. Now, we don't have to depend on them. The prospects come directly into Rock Hill.

"We took the right route after the mills closed down, developing Tech Park. And a lot of that credit goes to Joe Lanford. It's a New South City. There is no question about that! We are first class!

"We have fed off Charlotte like Gastonia has fed off Charlotte. We have been at the right place at the right time. Just because you are 25 miles from Charlotte doesn't mean you are going to be first class. It's the leadership, too. And we have had excellent leadership. It is unlimited what we will be in the future."

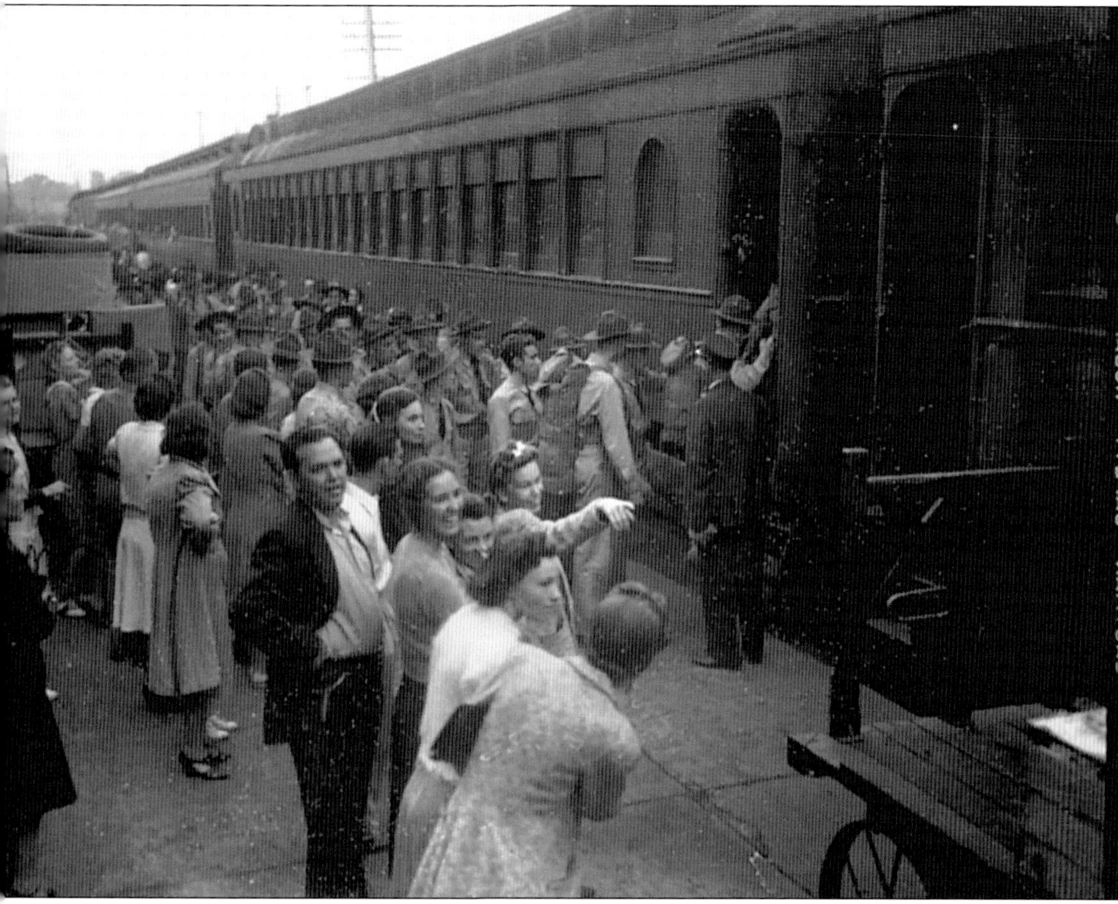

Troops prepare to leave Rock Hill for World War II service.

PEACEMAKER

Nearing the end of his long life, Wade Witherspoon paused to reflect on his service to Rock Hill and his years as an educator. Even near death, Mr. Witherspoon was dignified, articulate, and confident. It was these same qualities which helped him to be a calming voice in a volatile era. While other cities erupted in violence and hateful rhetoric, Mr. Witherspoon and others (Brother David Boone, for instance) guided the community toward integration. As the next chapter documents, however, there was some resistance to change, but Mr. Witherspoon guided the community toward integration. Witherspoon and his allies were, quite simply, peacemakers who looked beyond differences and sought common ground. As he once observed, "This town's not perfect. It's not likely to ever be, but then I'm not perfect, either."

"I was born in a house that sat on the corner of Reid Street and Wilson Street. My daddy bought that house about five years before I was born. I kept it until the city cut that underpass, and they offered me what they wanted. I told them that wasn't enough. They said that's what they were going to pay me. The house was 221 South Wilson. They changed it to 225 before I was married. I kept it until I was married.

"I worked two major jobs in my lifetime. I taught school the whole time. Only thing I ever did for 46 years.

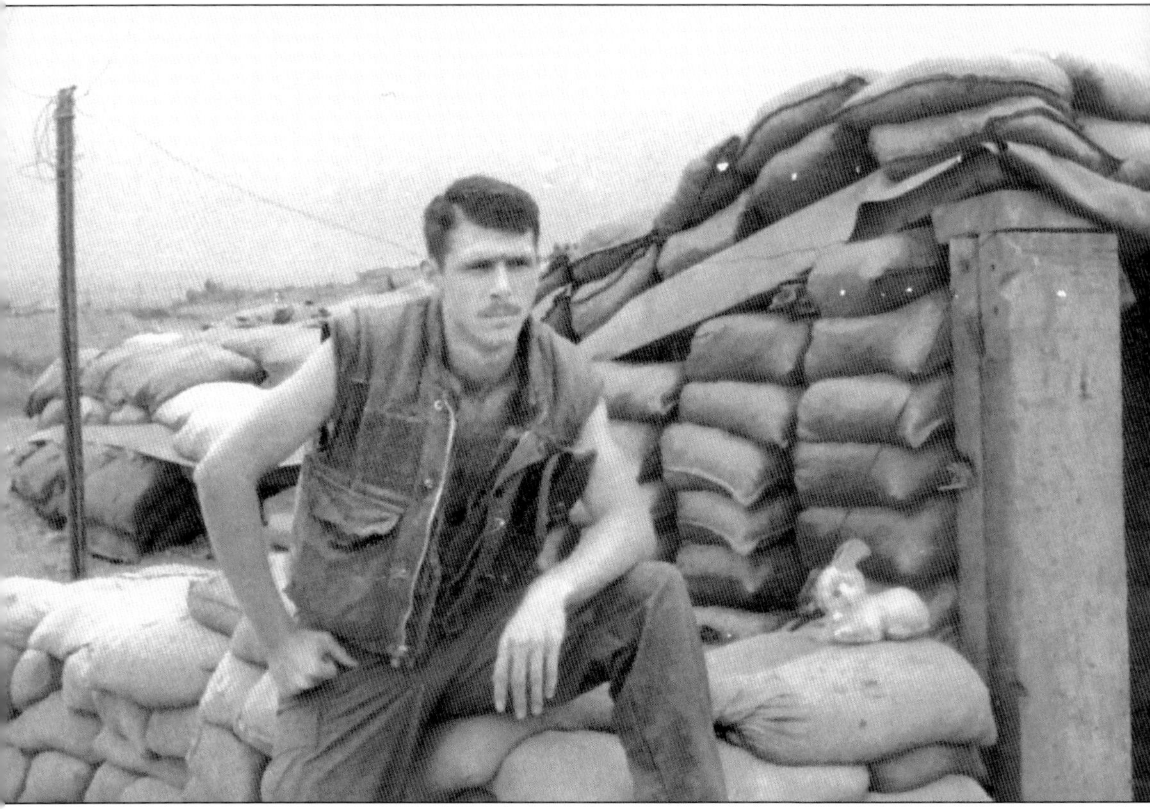

Rock Hill's sons and daughters have heeded the call of their nation in every war. Here is Phil Land in 1966.

"I guess you could say that I was a principal, under segregated circumstances, that I grew up mostly under; virtually all Negro schools. What they call "teaching principals." You get three or four people for the price of one and don't pay that one, you see. They give you a certificate to teach. You taught your classes, and they call you the principal of the school. That meant you were responsible for what was going on there, and my first job was as a teacher right here in the city of Rock Hill at what they called Emmett Scott. They're going to have a reunion down there this week...Scottites.... I named them Scottites. The reunion has been going on for some 15 or 16 years, I guess. Most people don't realize that a small, so-called "black school" would keep together that long, but they have. They've done a lot of good work. They've issued scholarships...One of the girls working on the newspaper in Myrtle Beach graduated from Emmett Scott. We had doctors, some of them turned out to be. I was a principal for a while. My year's salary the first year was $585.

"I taught at Emmett Scott. Well, I've taught in most of the schools in Rock Hill. I started teaching at Emmett Scott in 1930. I taught down there for seven years. I left there and went to Chester County. I taught in a school down there they called a high school. It was just a ramshakled two-story building. About four rooms to it. It was just a shack with no books. This was in 1937 I'm talking about. I stayed down there and got in touch with a lot of people and managed to get a school built, a nice brick school, and I stayed until I got the school accredited by the state. After it was state-accredited, I felt like I could leave there, but it took me 20 years

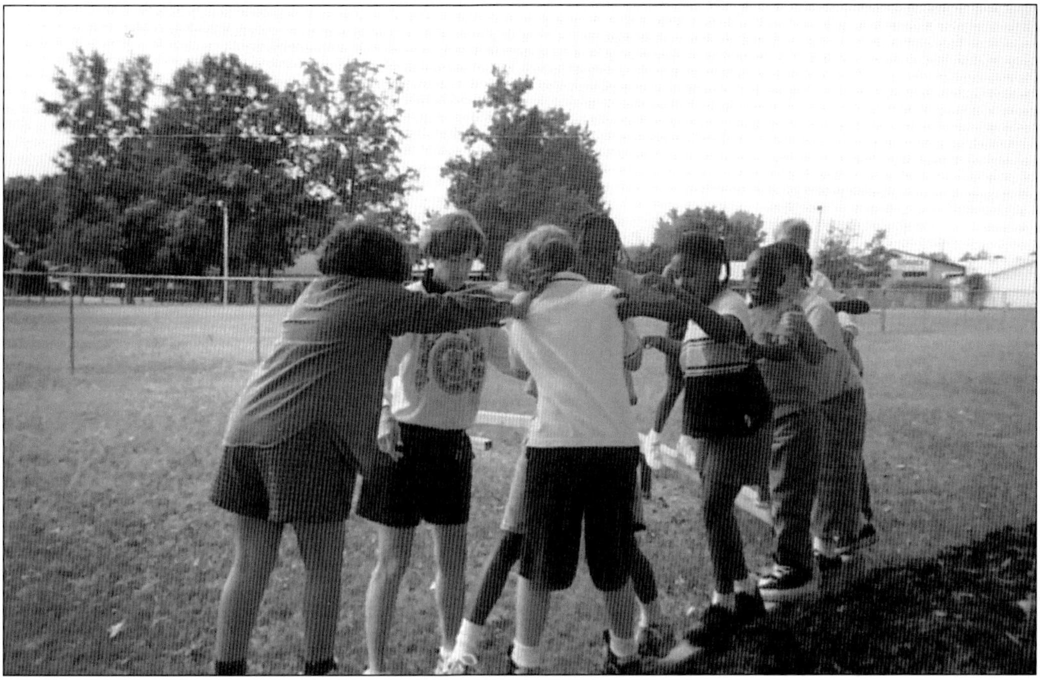

Richmond Drive Elementary School teacher Becky Bryant Faris (second from left) instructs her physical education students.

to do it. Then I came back to Rock Hill. Mr. Sullivan was superintendent when I came back. I came back to Rock Hill, and my first job was to take over a new school they were building at Castle Heights. And I was the first principal of Castle Heights school. There was no middle school. Then they transferred me from Castle Heights to another school over there. All these schools are still being operated. Edgewood. At that time Edgewood was the largest middle school in Rock Hill. They finally made it a special school and made me the principal of it again. Rock Hill did not have a vocational school. There wasn't a vocational school in this area. I was assistant director of the career development center, we called it. Sam Wooten was the director, and I was the assistant—the only one he had when he was getting it set up. Some of the kids I worked with over there at CDC got hold of a picture of mine, and before I knew anything about it had cards made up. I retired from CDC in 1976. My career was from 1930 til 1976.

"Well, after I finished S.C. State University, they call it now, in 1929, and 30 years later they came up with the idea, or already had the idea, that we weren't entitled to pay because we didn't know as much. I wasn't accepting that because I did know if I know what you want me to know, because I wanted to know what I wanted to know, too. And I never have known as much as I wanted to know. Never have and never will. Anyway, I went back to school and got a master's degree from Hampton University in Virginia. My wife had three degrees, got one from Benedict College in Columbia. She had one from Teacher's College in New York, a master's, and these are the ones the paper said didn't know enough to get paid. They paid me a third of what everybody else who had half my education...formal training. That wasn't always pleasant to think about. I was lucky to have some teachers who thought along those lines. And they made a bigger impression. One was from Morehouse College in Atlanta.

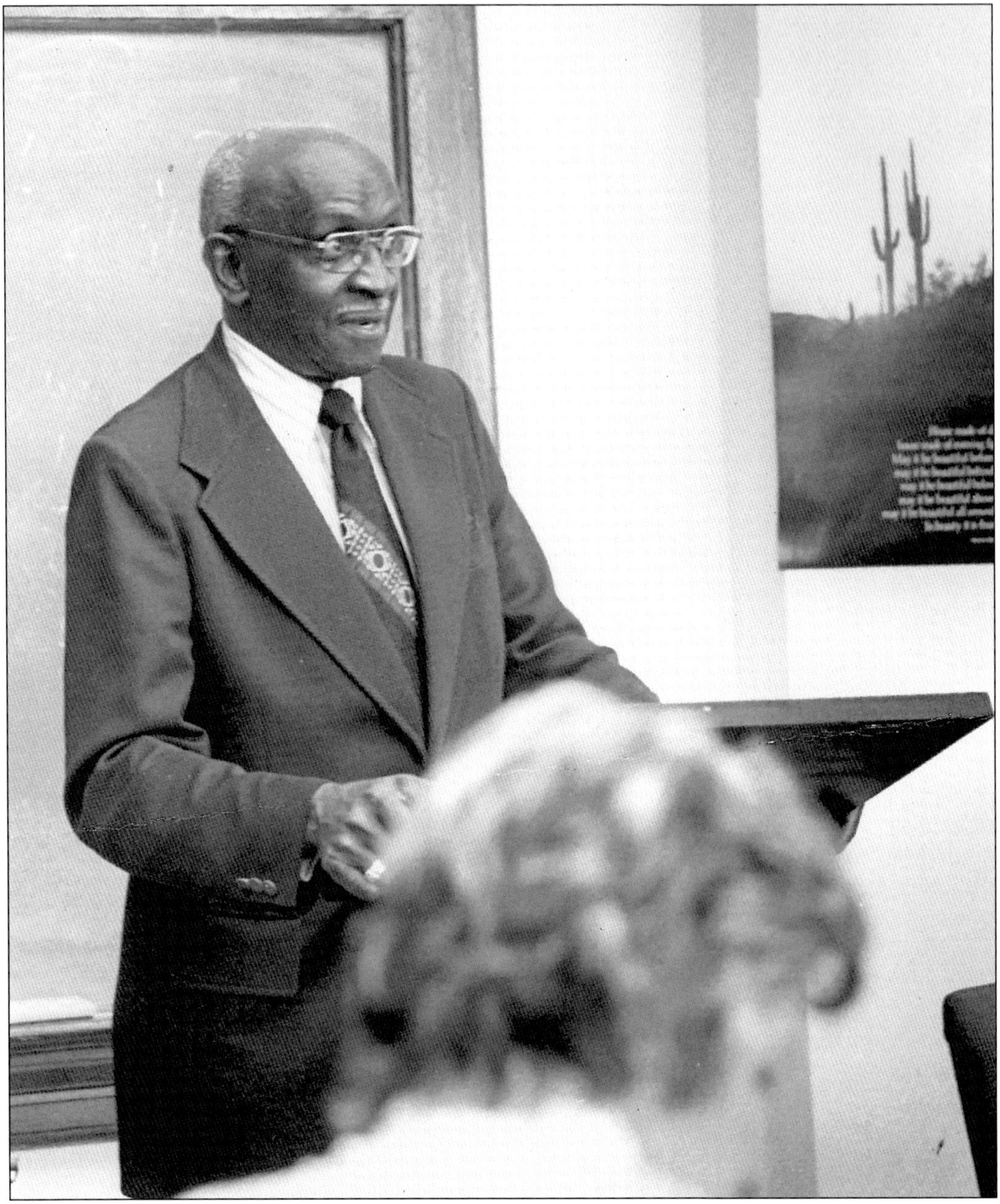

Wade Hampton Witherspoon, peacemaker, is shown here in 1977.

"The President of Morehouse College was one of my teachers when I was coming along. He himself went to the same college and came back later, and I happened to catch him there, when he was teaching there. He was one of the greatest...You can name the president of Harvard, Yale, Oxford, and all the rest. There weren't any greater than Dr. Benny Mayes.

"Well, Martin Luther King attended Morehouse, you know. Mayes was his teacher, too. Weren't many greater. And anything you saw in writing and wrote for Dr. Mayes, he wanted you to be exact. He would stand no writing or anything that you'd submit to him that you didn't give credit to anybody that you quoted. He called that plagiarism. He called it 'literary thieving.' I'll never forget, one boy told on another who was getting a better grade, that had copied some things, and Dr. Mayes thought that whatever he had copied from somewhere that he was doing pretty well to think like that. Dr. Mayes said, 'What did you say? Did you say that he had copied this from something?' And the boy showed him where he had copied from. The boy's name was Sam Washington. Dr. Mayes told him right there in class, 'Mr. Washington, after all I have told you about plagiarism, literary thieving, and yet you would do a thing like this? Copying from someone else without giving that person credit for it? No zero is big enough for you! You deserve a zero within a zero.'

"Well, in the city of Rock Hill, not only education particularly, almost any way you look I have had some service. I was appointed to the board of education in York County twice by Governor Dick Riley. I talked with him quite a lot. It's not a matter of writing letters back and forth. He'd sit down and talk just like we're talking.

"I was one of the lucky ones. I signed my name 'W.H. Witherspoon.' Those initials stand for Wade Hampton. My daddy was known around town as 'Hamp Witherspoon.' He worked for a man who was one of the leading bankers in this area. By area, I mean the Piedmont area. He lived in Rock Hill, and his name was Richard Lee Kerr. My dad worked for him. Took care of his horses and all the things around his house and all. Kept them in good shape that people just stand on the street and watch him pass. Had a harness, everything metal on the harness was solid brass. He kept it shining. Horses cleaned up. He was one of those. He curried horses if they didn't work that day. Horses got brushed and curried every day. I've never known him to work for anyone but himself. He had a business, hauled stuff for people. Everything went by train. And then he entered agreements or contracts with some of the stores uptown. Something come in at the express office or depot, and he'd take it to the store for them. It kept him pretty busy. A lot of people are surprised to find that farming is one thing that I know less about than anything I can imagine. I never farmed, never lived on a farm. Nearest I ever lived on a farm was over there on South Wilson Street where I was born. When I moved back to Rock Hill after I left Chester County, following 20 years, I moved in this house. I've been here now about 40 years.

"My mother and father believed in education! If the school was going to be open, we'd be there. That was the rule for all the children. And that was at a time when that was not common. Rock Hill didn't do much in big farming like they did in the lower part of the state. We did more manufacturing. We had cotton mills, made cloth, gingham. I woke up and went to sleep with the sound of the mills.

"When I got my master's degree at Hampton, everybody had to write a thesis, and they had to be accepted by a committee. But in some of the other schools that had been going on longer, you could take some extra hours; couldn't take extra house at Hampton. You wrote a thesis, and it had to be accepted. You'd go before the thesis committee, and they'd ask you questions about it.

"Another thing that we don't do that has been a harm to education. People came up with the idea of teacher tests. The teacher test was not designed primarily to make teachers betters in S.C. The teacher test was designed primarily to try to prove that Negro teachers didn't know as much as white teachers and shouldn't be paid as much. I was in the middle of it. All I did was for publicity's sake. I said that it wasn't true, and they found out that it wasn't. Because if it had been, why would they be jumping up and down and talking about children are illiterate? If they got rid of all those no good Negro teachers, there should be no illiteracy in America, none. We've got the mechanical equipment, books, and books should be the foundation of it. We are still going to have to go back to books; computers are not going to do it.

"Carhartt overalls were made right here in Rock Hill. Then another mill came in that made overalls, Blue Buckle. Carhartt overalls had brass buttons on it, ones that looked like a streetcar, in the shape of a streetcar. Some people wore those things when they dressed up. They liked them, and I've seen people wear Carhartt and Blue Buckle to church. It was a car like a railroad car or streetcar and made in the shape of a heart. I think the man's name was Carhartt.

"You could find enough to do. My mother was an expert washerwoman. She didn't leave home to do it. None of us left home to do anything that my parents felt would not be helpful. I have known towns in this area where they would close the schools early at cotton-picking time and try to get as many children as possible. Somebody come by and pick them up, take them to pick cotton from dawn to dusk, bring them back to town from out in the country where they had been. But I never did that in my life. None of us did.

"My daddy didn't stop me to do his work, and he didn't stop you to do anybody else's work. And both of my parents could read. I don't know where they got their formal training, but they could read and write. Most of their business papers they signed themselves and no 'making a mark.' You've heard of 'making a mark.'

"I had two sisters and one brother I didn't know; he died in infancy. I grew up with two sisters. I was the only one who went to a four-year college. See, we had Friendship College here, Clinton College here, and many of the churches… and that's something that hasn't been put in books as much as it should. One of the reasons for the differences as I see it, in the thinking between whites and so-called non-whites, is that some whites believe that non-whites were given special advantages, but not necessarily true. All the little churches had schools. The first school I attended in Rock Hill was not furnished by the state or the city. It was a little Episcopal school, over on West Black Street. You know the corner of Wilson and Black there was an Episcopal school. Hermon Presbyterian Church, right over here, had a little school in the back. At a lot of the rural area churches there were schools. A lot of times, the churches paid the teachers what they could. Sometimes the community chipped in a little.

"I was there when Emmett Scott was built, too. They had finished building Emmett Scott, and they finished it near Christmas time, in the fall of the year. And as soon as they got enough of it finished and enough old desks made for the children to sit on, we started moving in from these little church schools and around. And it was on the edge of what they called a sewage bed. And all the raw sewage that I know, of or hear, of in Rock Hill was buried in open ditches back there. Students had to live with that, and the people who had to live in that area had to live with that. The sewage bed was near the school. The school was built almost out of town. It was in the southernmost part of town. The city limits weren't but a couple of blocks from where the school was built.

"People change. If people don't change, things don't change. What I'm saying is that Rock Hill seemingly became a little bit more liberal when people began to realize that there were other people in town who helped to make the town what it was. Some folks believed that the man at the top makes the town. Not necessarily. Sometimes, the man down here makes the change. The so-called 'black codes' that they had all over the south; some of the codes were so strict on the law that a Negro couldn't have a book in his house. Nobody was supposed to sell them a book or give them a book or let him read one on the premises. You couldn't have property.

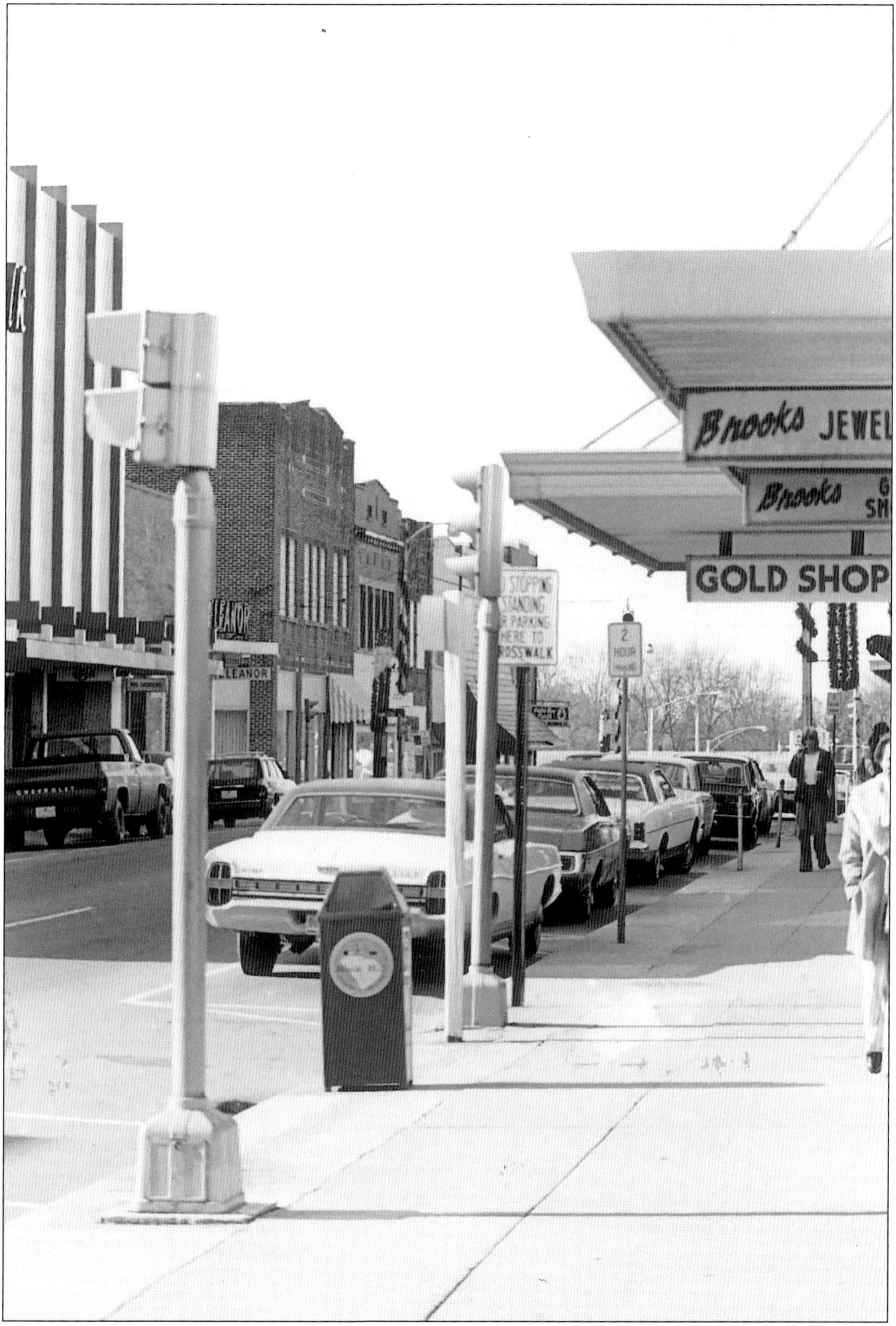

By the early 1970s, Rock Hill had become an All America City, and segregation had ended.

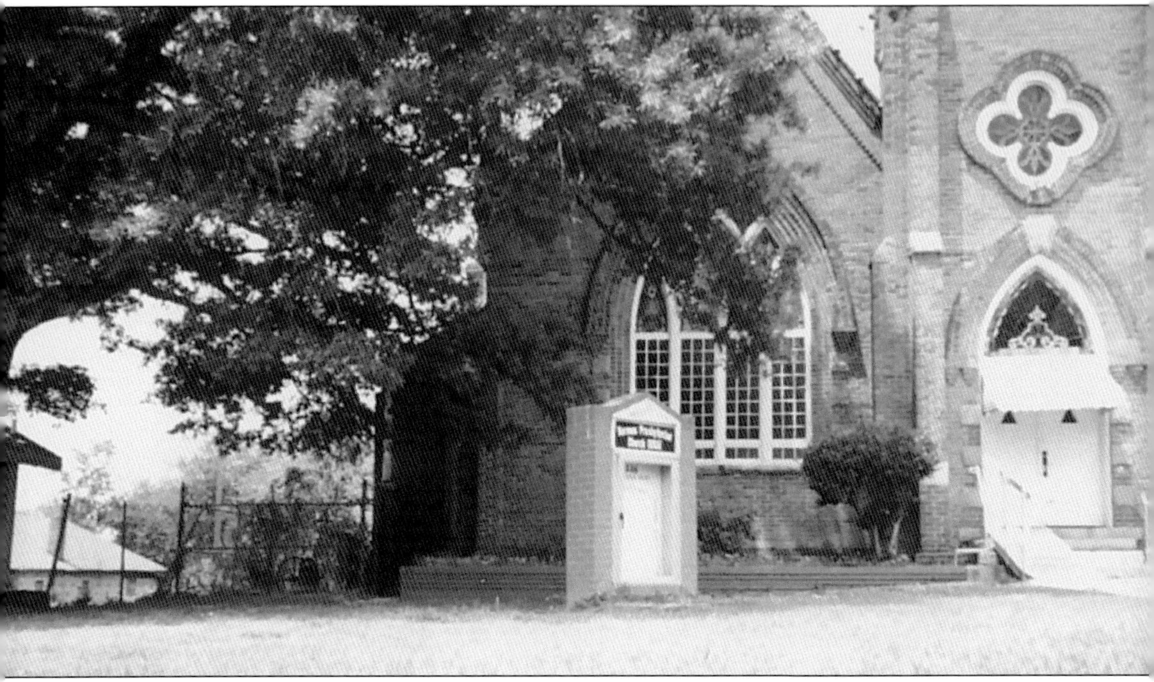

Hermon Presbyterian Church was a beacon in the Civil Rights Movement.

He couldn't, if anybody mistreated him and broke the law that was strictly found that a Negro could hardly bring suit against him for any retribution because he wasn't supposed to have sense enough to know that. But they did know it.

"Some of the biggest changes, I guess, took place around the Charleston area. One of the richest men in S.C. at one time was a Negro. Something you don't see a whole lot written around about. That's because we have not written history. I think history should be a factual account of what happened. They've gotten different kinds of historians, they call them now. Interpretive historians who, instead of just giving the facts of a situation, they tell you what they think that people thought when they did that. You can't tell what a man thought when it happened. In too many instances, history has not been recorded. And if it was recorded, it was never given much thought and attention. The result is that a lot of people growing up and making decisions without the information necessary to make a proper decision. If you don't have the information on what happened, how are you going to make a proper decision on something that might happen again? And things did happen again. It's happening now, the Ku Klux Klan, for example, and the burning of black churches.

"One of my favorite Bible verses, can't remember chapter and all, is 'What does the lord require of thee? Three things: to do justice, to have mercy and to walk humbly.' I have tried to be faithful to that Scripture.

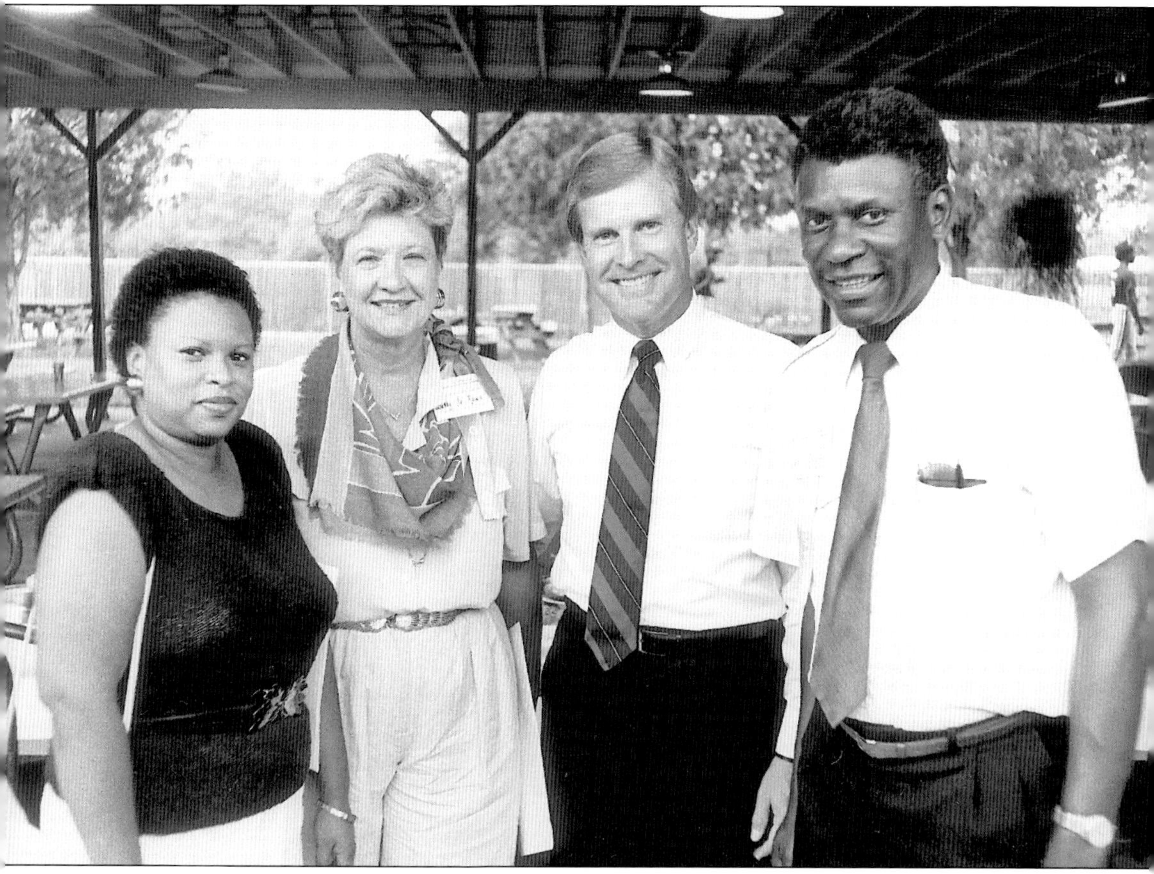

Governor Carroll Campbell visited Rock Hill in the late 1980s.

FRIENDSHIP NINE

As the decade of the 1960s dawned, winds of change swept across the South. Mass boycotts and peaceful protests were being used to focus that nation's attention on the injustice of "separate but equal." Civil Rights organizations, such as the Student Non-Violent Coordinating Committee (SNCC), the National Association for the Advancement of Colored People (NAACP), the Southern Christian Leadership Conference (SCLC), and the Congress of Racial Equality (CORE), argued for a new day in race relations in the country.

A new tactic in this holy war against segregation was the sit-in demonstration at restaurant lunch counters. By early 1961, these sit-ins had come to Rock Hill, conducted by a group of courageous Friendship College students unwilling to accept discrimination. Below, Deann Bice Segal, the holder of a history master's degree, shares her research on the arrival of these sit-ins to our city.

"On the eve of the first anniversary of the 1960 sit-in in Greensboro, nine Friendship College students and Thomas Gaither of the Congress of Racial Equality, accompanied by five women, began to picket McCrory's store on Main Street. Around 11:30 a.m. on January 31, 1961, Gaither and the students entered the store and sat at the lunch counter. They refused to leave when asked to do so and were immediately arrested for trespassing. The entire Rock Hill Police Force was on duty that morning, and present at the arrest was the chief of the South Carolina Law Enforcement Division and five SLED officers. Willie McCleod, Charles Taylor, James Wells, Clarance Graham, David Williamson, Robert McCullough, Mack Workman, W.T. Massey, John Gaines, and Gaither were each placed under $100 bond. After a night in jail, the young men were brought to trial in the Recorder's Court and fined by Judge Billy D. Hayes $100 or 30 days in jail. They chose to remain in jail rather than post the bond.

"The Rock Hill protesters were sent to the segregated York County Prison Farm to serve their sentences on a work crew, at hard labor. McCrory's lunch counter remained closed. The Woolworth's counter had been closed for weeks. Caravans from the college traveled to the prison to give moral support to the students. Their prison sentences gained national attention and was reported in *Time, Ebony, Newsweek,* and *Jet* magazines.

"On February 6, four SNCC activists staged a sit-in at Good's Drug Store in Rock Hill. Arrested, convicted, and sentenced to 30 days in jail were Joseph Jones, Charles Sherrod, Ruby Smith, and Dianne Nash, all out-of-state college students. The police vowed to uphold trespassing laws, and SNCC called for activists to make Rock Hill a focal point for the demonstrations. SNCC executive secretary Edward King called on all with the same moral convictions as the students to go to Rock Hill and 'join them at the lunch counter and in jail.'

"An early SNCC newsletter details the arrests in Rock Hill and reported that the students had been placed on bread and water and placed in solitary confinement due to staging a work stoppage. SNCC claimed the work stoppage was due to the protesters having to do twice as much as another crew, but Winfred Cross, in an article in the *Evening Herald,* January 31, 1986, reported that an unattended muscle injury to John Gaines resulted in the work stoppage. The students refused to work until Gaines was helped and, as a result, were placed in solitary confinement. The group stayed in a 9-by-9 cell, refusing even bread and water, for three days until Gaines returned.

"Editorials on the demonstrations in the *Evening Herald* were surprisingly benign. One published February 6, 1961, advocated careful study of the race question and a long planning period for possible solutions. Stating that social revolution takes much time, the editor warned that waiting too long or pushing too fast would cause a crisis. Another editorial from February 8 decried the fact that Rock Hill, well known as one of the most liberal and progressive South Carolina cities, had been chosen as the focal point for the sit-ins. Warning that the nation would be watching what happened here, the editors advocated that law and order must prevail. They praised the police for the effective handling of the many demonstrations and protests held in town, and lauded the citizens for not allowing any 'regrettable incidents' to occur.

"On February 7, 1961, the Committee for the Promotion of Human Rights hosted a meeting in which members of CORE, SNCC, the NAACP, and other activist groups addressed a crowd of about 300 African Americans in Rock Hill. The Reverend C.A. Ivory, local president of the NAACP and head of the Committee for the Protection of Human Rights, discussed the arrests of the Friendship students, called for more student picketing and boycotts by the black community. The next day, there were an estimated 100 people picketing around town, and a white man joined the protests.

"A group of supporters from Tennessee Agriculture and Industrial College in Nashville arrived in Rock Hill to show their support for the students and to help with the demonstrations. Protesters staged a two-hour demonstration downtown on Saturday and a 'kneel-in' in white churches on Sunday. They were admitted to three

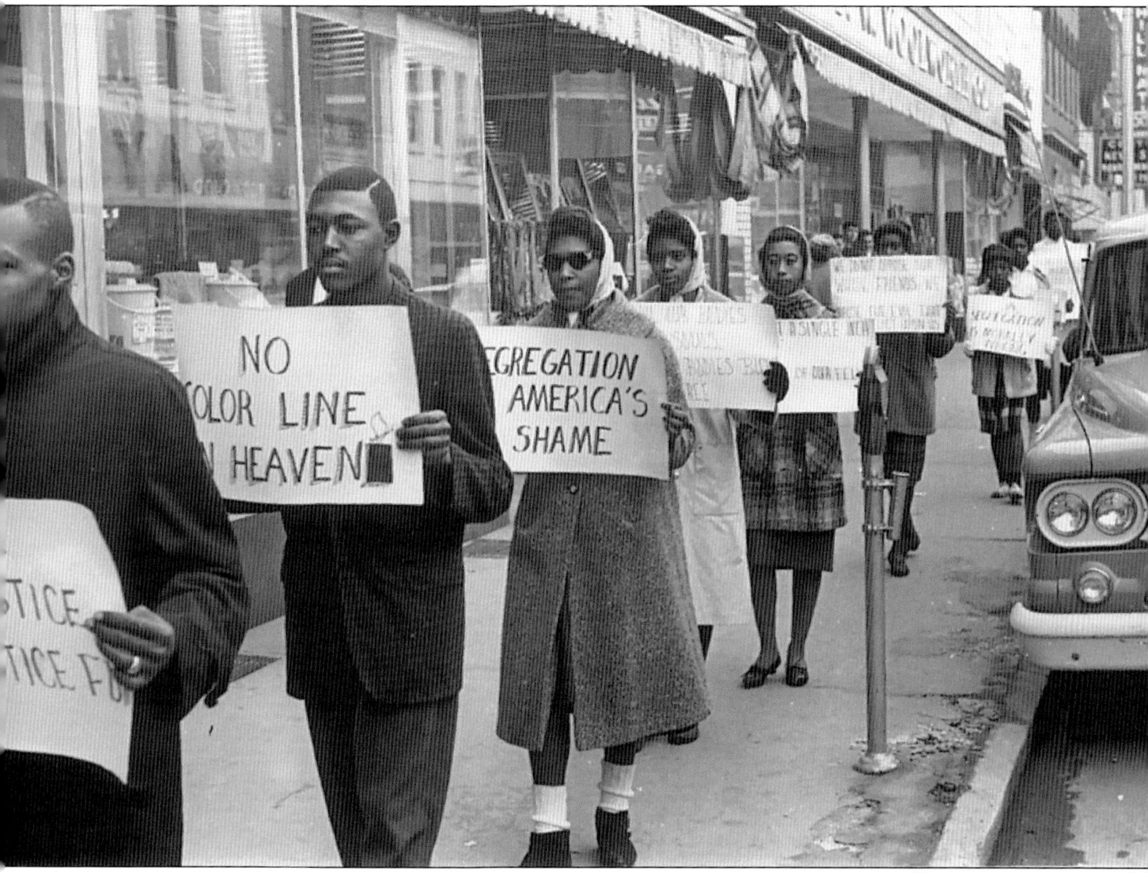

After the arrest of the Friendship Nine, peaceful protesters focused the nation's attention on racism in Rock Hill.

and turned away from at least two.

"The student protesters did not only have to confront hostile white supremacists in their protests. They also had to overcome opposition from the more established activist groups and the black middle class. The jailed activists hoped others would join them in Rock Hill, but funds were scarce, parents objected, and school officials, some of whom owed their jobs to white administrators, were pressured to discipline long absences.

"The Friendship Nine served a total of 28 days. They were released early, according to James Wells, now a Rock Hill attorney, because officials heard a large welcoming party would be meeting to greet the students on their official release date. The student activists did not achieve their goal of mass demonstrations in Rock Hill. The active involvement of the many civil rights groups in the Friendship action demonstrated a widespread willingness for direct action and brought a sense of cohesion to the movement.

"The sit-ins were only partially successful in integrating Southern lunch counters. Mr. Wells remembers that McCrory's closed for a few years after the sit-in, but when it reopened, it had an integrated counter. The civil rights demonstrations were often put down by whites as the work of 'outside agitators,' but as black activism spread, spurred by courageous acts like those of the Friendship Nine, white Rock Hill was forced to look at its tradition of segregation reflected in the faces of its black citizens."

Westminister

One summer morning, the editors visited some of the residents at Westminister Retirement Home. The recollections of these senior adults add much depth to our understanding of this diverse community. Among the people with whom we spoke were the first out-of-state woman to enroll at Winthrop and Dr. Allen Edwards, the former chairperson of Winthrop's Sociology Department. They, and a room full of others, provided valuable insight into the forces that shaped Rock Hill. Often, people came to our city for educational, personal, or professional opportunities, but then they never left.

"My name is Losina Walker, and I was the first out-of-state girl to attend Winthrop. Dr. Roberts was head of the Music Department, and that was his first year here. He called Papa and said, 'If you'll let Losina attend Winthrop, her music won't cost her anything, because I'll use her as the product of my teaching.'

"I lived with Dr. Roberts and his wife. They had rented the old Peter Airy House. Because I lived out in town, I didn't have to wear the uniform, except when I was on campus. One was short-sleeved. We all had white collars; that's for everyday, or we could wear it other places but not for dress-up. For dress-up occasions, we wore a twill navy-blue wool, and, oh lord, we had to wear black hose with black shoes, and we all had the same little hat. It was small with a sort of rolled-up brim.

I entered Winthrop in the fall of 1925. Well, I first had to ask Dr. D.B. Johnson (He lived two years after that.). I asked him, told him, that I wanted to go to Winthrop. He was nice, but he said they didn't admit anybody to Winthrop except South Carolina girls, maybe a few from North Carolina, because Winthrop was supported by South Carolina taxes. So I wrote back to him, and I told him that I didn't depend on the taxpayers and that I would be living downtown with Dr. Roberts.

"Well, the Roberts family rented the old Peter Airy House, and it was about a block off Milton Avenue. So, we could walk to Winthrop, but it was just as good if you could find a ride. I wore Winthrop uniforms, being downtown I could wear the other, and I sang in the First Presbyterian Church. Do you happen to remember Charlie Cobb? He was downtown people's banker, and my first Sunday in Rock Hill I sang at the First Presbyterian Church, sang a solo, and he got in touch with me the next day, and he said to me 'Well, now I know the minister, his sermon, was taken from Kings, but I was thinking Queen.' Anyway, that was my introduction to Charlie Cobb. Anyway, I sang as a soloist there throughout the winter. I got $50 a month for my services.

"I was born in Missouri but raised in Oklahoma. So, my mother and my father were both physicians and surgeons, and they decided to settle in Blackwell, Oklahoma. We lived up over the bank. At that time, there were three banks and then one clothing store for women's clothes.

"I was a long way from home, but of course, my family knew Dr. Roberts. We met him during his first year at Enid, Oklahoma, as head of the Music Department, and Papa wanted me to be a physician, but I thought we had enough of those in the family. So I joined Dr. Roberts in Rock Hill.

"When I was at Winthrop, I was known as Elizabeth Youngblood. I was born in Plant City, Florida, but my parents died when I was young, and I came to Rock Hill to live with some relatives when I was eight years old. So, I've been here since I was eight. So, I'm from Rock Hill!

"I remember the tornado of 1926. I was walking down Hope Street that goes into the Marion Street neighborhood. This

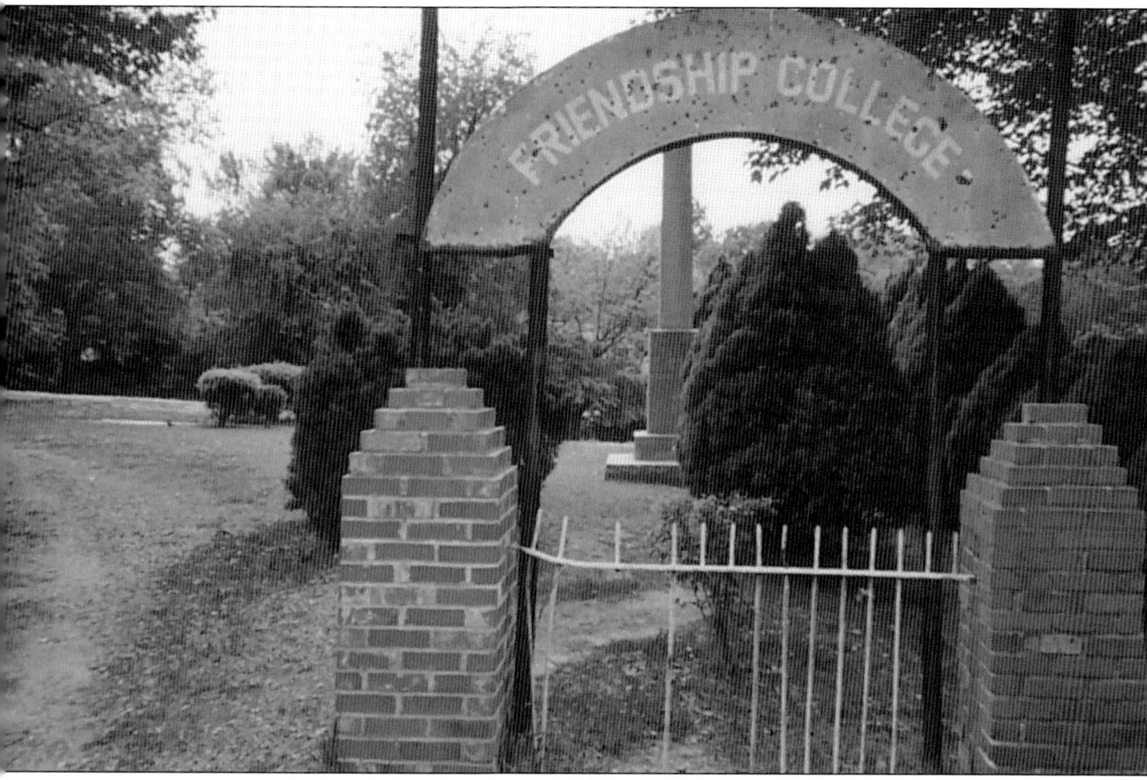

Small Friendship College provided many of the young men and women who questioned segregation.

friend of mine, we were walking down there the day after Thanksgiving, and we saw this terrible cloud. And she knew a lady, a Mrs. Vicker, who lived on Hope Street, and we went in there to ask her could we stay until after the storm. And we were in the dining room that had triple windows, and she said, 'I think we better go into the living room.' And all those windows were blown out. You know, we felt like we were saved."

"I'm Dr. Allan Edwards. And I know before we came to Rock Hill, as I recall, we were at Clemson. I had been teaching there for a couple of years. This was 1942 to 1944. We were staying at Oconee State Park for a week, and I came over to Winthrop because they had a vacancy as chairman of the Sociology Department, and they offered me the job. I turned it down. Dr. Henry Sims, the president, called after that and asked me why. I gave him two reasons, and he met both of them, so I just had to come to Rock Hill.

"There are three groups of people in Rock Hill. There are the people in business, there are the executives in the mills here, and there are the Winthrop faculty. Now, there are three groups. They constitute probably less than ten percent of all the people in Rock Hill.

"We arrived here in 1944. We lived in the college apartments. It's where the Thompson Dormitory and Cafeteria is now. We had an upstairs apartment, 326 York Avenue, for five years and a downstairs apartment for six years before we built our house on Mary Dale Lane.

"One thing about being on campus, you know, was at Clemson, we had families there, but in Rock Hill, most of the faculty were women, single women, and there were relatively few men. Dr. Jarrell said

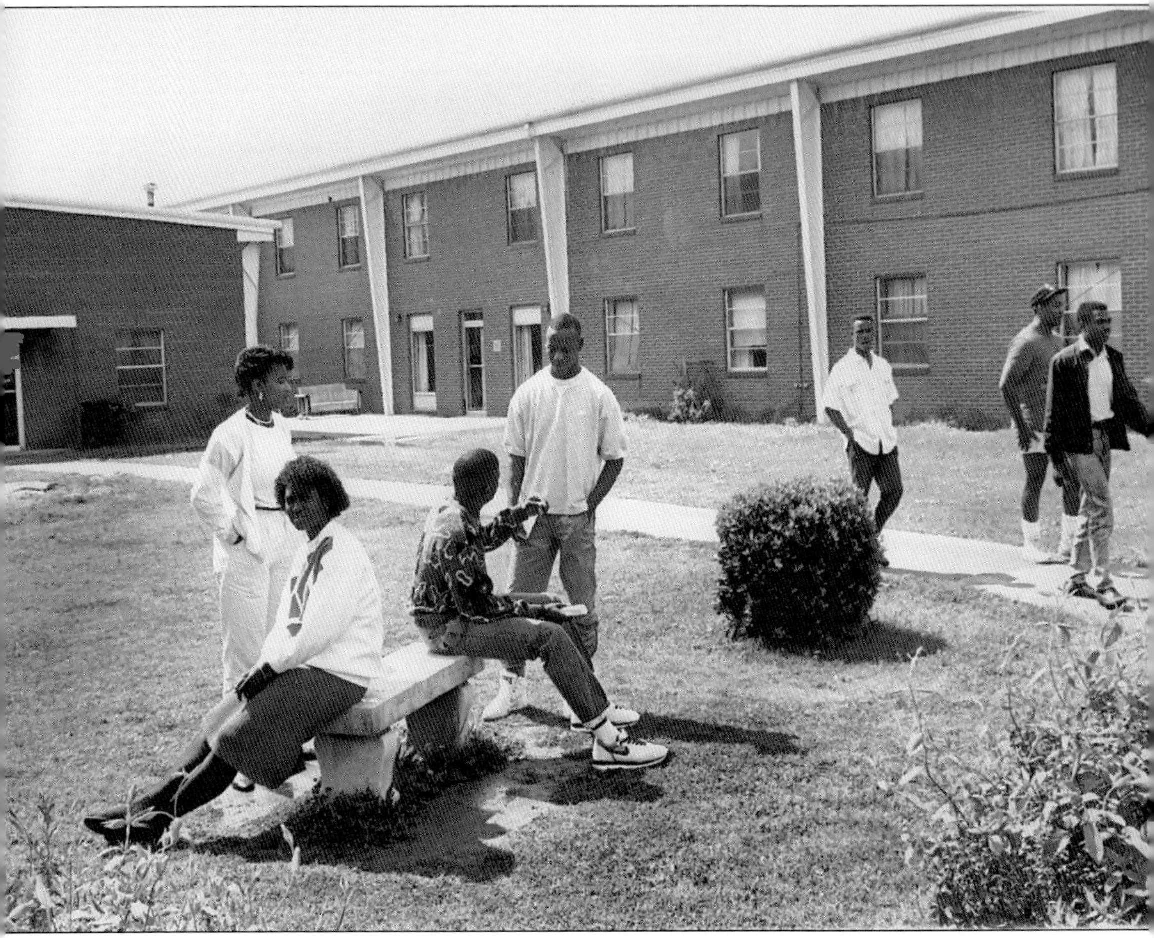

that he and his wife had to apologize when they had a child. They had one daughter and had to apologize because people didn't have children. Perhaps that's an exaggeration, but that's sort of the way it was."

"I'm Virginia Whiteside. I was born and grew up in the lower part of SC, a tiny little village called Greelyville. My father was a farmer, but he had read about Dr. D.B. Johnson, and he had two daughters, so he decided that they were going to Winthrop. We both are graduates of Winthrop. But, anyway, I finished high school in 1926, and in the early summer, I came to Winthrop. It was a much different looking place than it is now. Everybody didn't have a car then, so I had to ride the train from the lower part of the state into Camden, and then I got another train and came on to Rock Hill and drove right up on the back campus. I came up and was looking, and there were at least 15 or 22 horse wagons lined up right where the train stopped. Most of them were black men, and there were two mules or two horses hitched to each wagons. Then the train crew started putting our trunks into the wagons. Then we followed the wagons up to the dormitories.

"I was in Catawba Dormitory. The first one we came to. That's still on campus. And Mrs. Tutwilter was our matron. She was a tiny little old lady and just as sweet as she could be, but she meant for you to do just by the rules. We had a copy of them. They would seem funny to you now, but anyway, we could not have a date unless

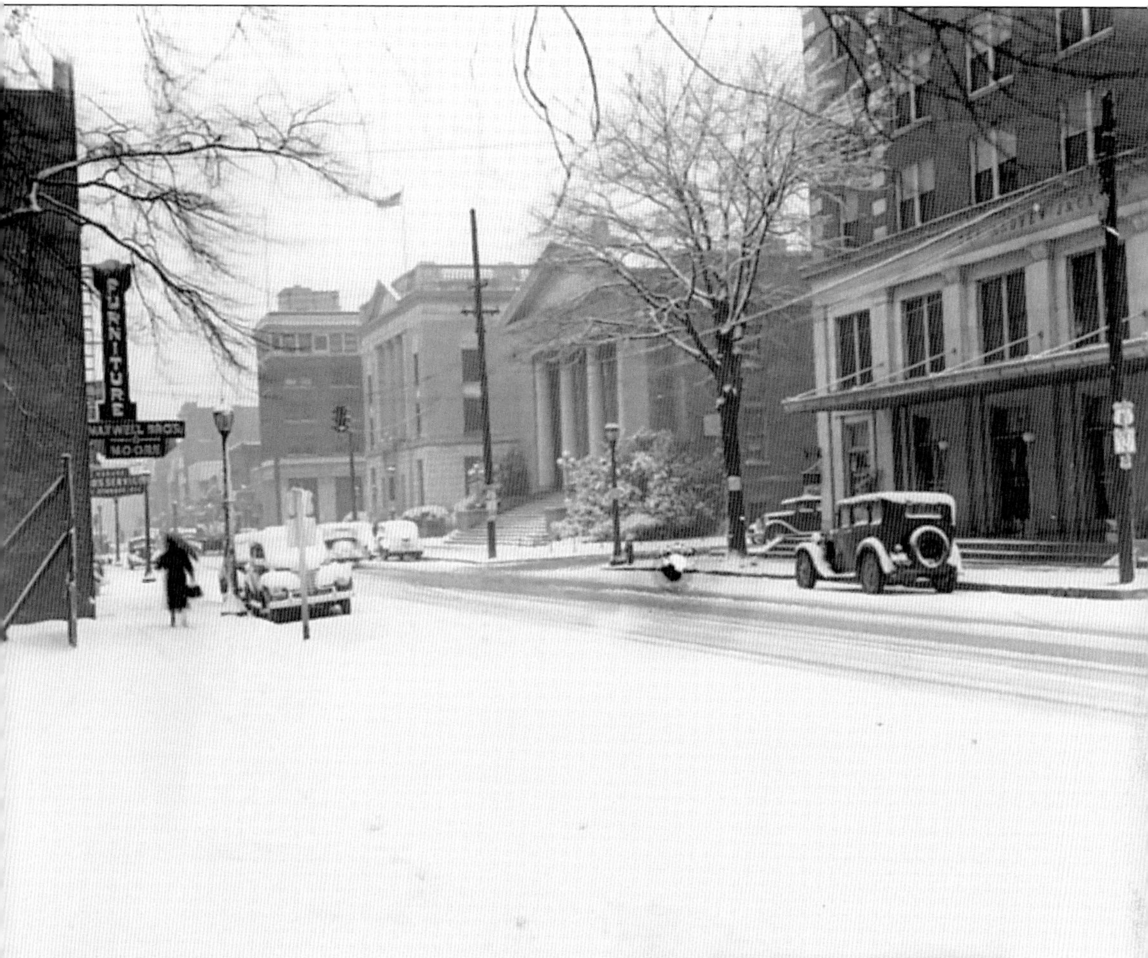

This photograph shows a snowy winter day in front of the Andrew Jackson Hotel.

our matron were sitting in the parlor with us or in the next room with all the doors open. But you could walk on the campus if you had a brother visit you. Somehow, all the girls had brothers!

"I was there during the Depression, and everybody was very careful. Of course, so many of us had fathers who were farmers. That meant plenty to eat but very little to spend. I tell my grandchildren now that if I had a pencil, no matter how long or how short, I didn't buy another. They say, 'Grandmother, that was just a nickel.' I say, 'Honey, I didn't have the nickel.' And then I remember that we always saved up our money when we went to town, which we tried to do as often as we could. We'd always stop at Good's Drug Store and get an ice cream soda. But anyway, we had a lot of sadness during that year. Dr. D.B. Johnson was there when we got to Winthrop College, and he was always very careful about everybody being exactly in uniform. We had two dresses, see? We had a silk one for summer and a wool navy blue. It was all navy blue for winter. I had to wear these white collars. You better have on a white collar and not a colored tie and tie it around your neck. We all were afraid of the dean. She would ride up and down the streets in the college car, and she was always watching, particularly for

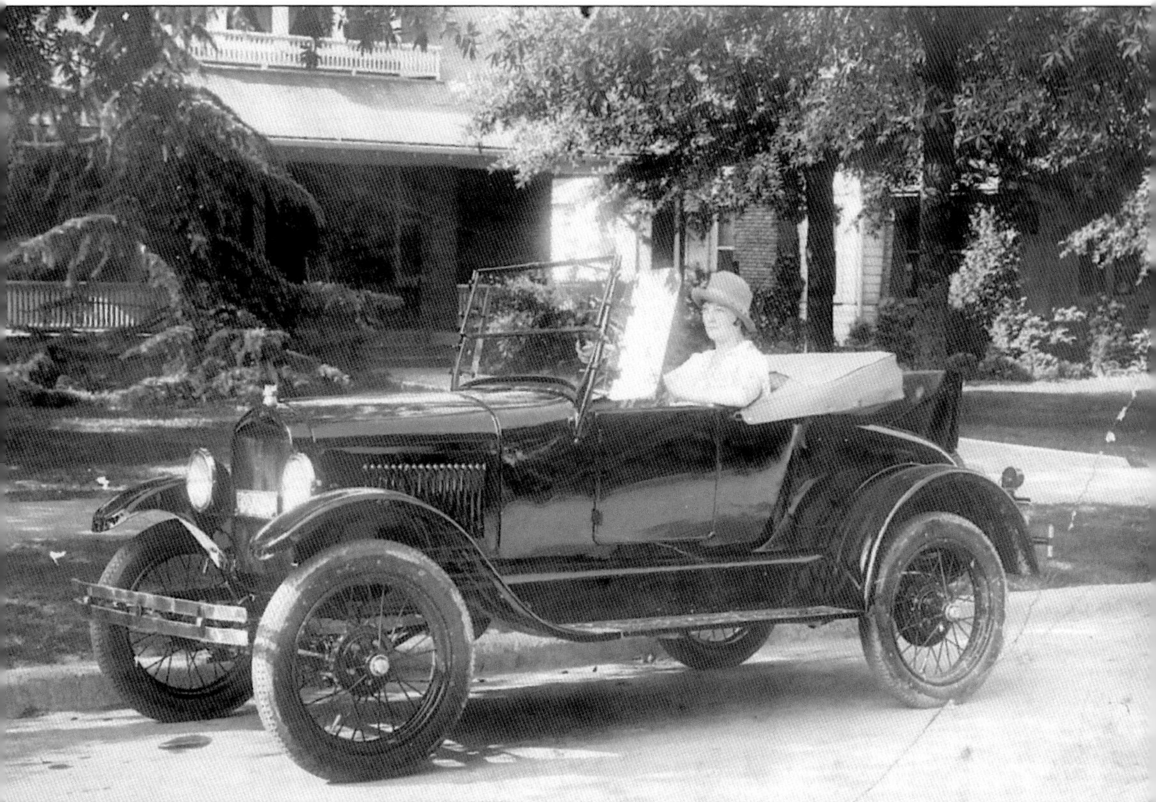

the ones who were not in strict uniform. And on Sunday morning, to be sure we did not get out of uniform, we had to line up at the door of our dormitory, and the matrons came to see if we had on gun metal hose. I don't mean thin, a little bit off, but they had to be black; so one of those dresses and white collar, and then we had hats. You should have seen the hats. They were really comical. All shapes, but they were navy hats with a little band around.

"And we got through that year. Now we all did not go home for Thanksgiving because our first semester ended the day before Thanksgiving, and the day after Thanksgiving we had exams. So nobody went home, particularly the ones who had to ride the train back home. There were a few whose parents had a car and could go maybe for one day. When Christmas came, everybody was ready to go home that first year. We all went home on time. It was a very few days until we heard that our dear Dr. Johnson had passed away. We read it in the paper. So when we came back after Christmas, it was a sad lot of girls, because we loved him. He was very popular. Every day, from the time we came until he passed away, he had chapel in the little chapel in main building. It was required. We had to attend chapel, and he always talked to us. He would read the Bible, have a prayer, and then he would tell us some of the local news on the campus or maybe some national news that he would like for us to know. He was buried on campus, and probably all of you know that, later on, he was moved to the little place that was brought from Columbia here, that was the first Winthrop College.

"I graduated in 1930, and then I thought, 'What am I going to do? I don't have a job.' But I roomed with this girl who lived in Bullock's Creek, and her mother knew about two vacancies in schools; one was in Smyra, and one was in Hickory Grove, and she said, 'Now girls, get ready in the

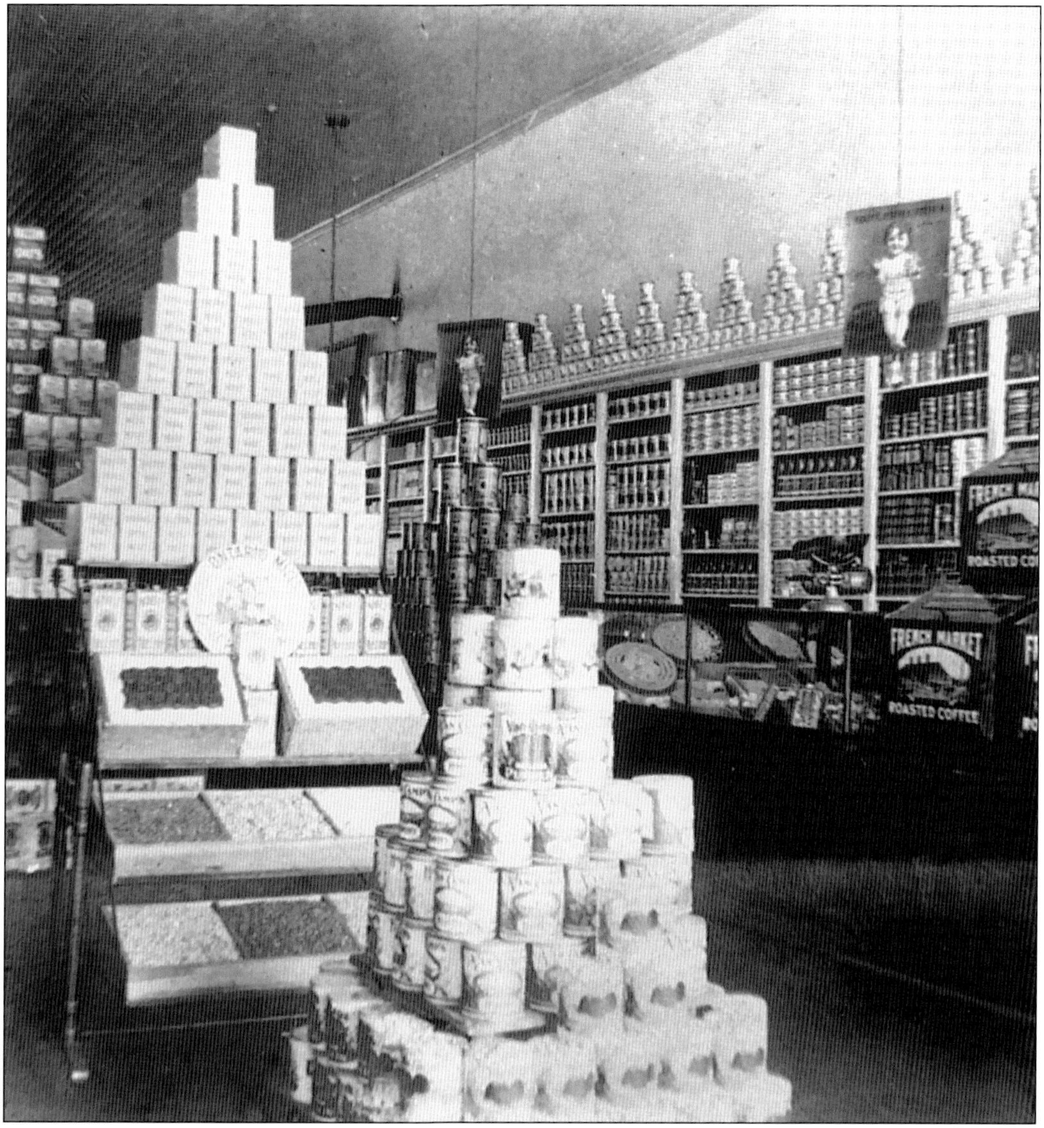

The Rock Hill Supply Company is pictured here in the 1920s.

morning. We're going to get the horse and the buggy, and we're going to get you those jobs.' So, we got ready, and I don't know whether we got the jobs or she got the jobs for us. But we got them. This friend of mine was a primary teacher and I taught the 7th and 8th grades. And we were so happy to have that work. I got $74 a month, and I had gotten two or three months checks, and I put them in the little bank in Sharon, and that's when all the banks closed. Oh, and I had to say a prayer because my bank didn't close. I still had the three checks. While I was there teaching, I met this young man, and we married. And then we moved to Rock Hill. He was a school teacher, too. I'm still living in Rock Hill, and it's been a wonderful place to live. I've met so many wonderful people.

"We lived out at the country club. We bought an old house. You may

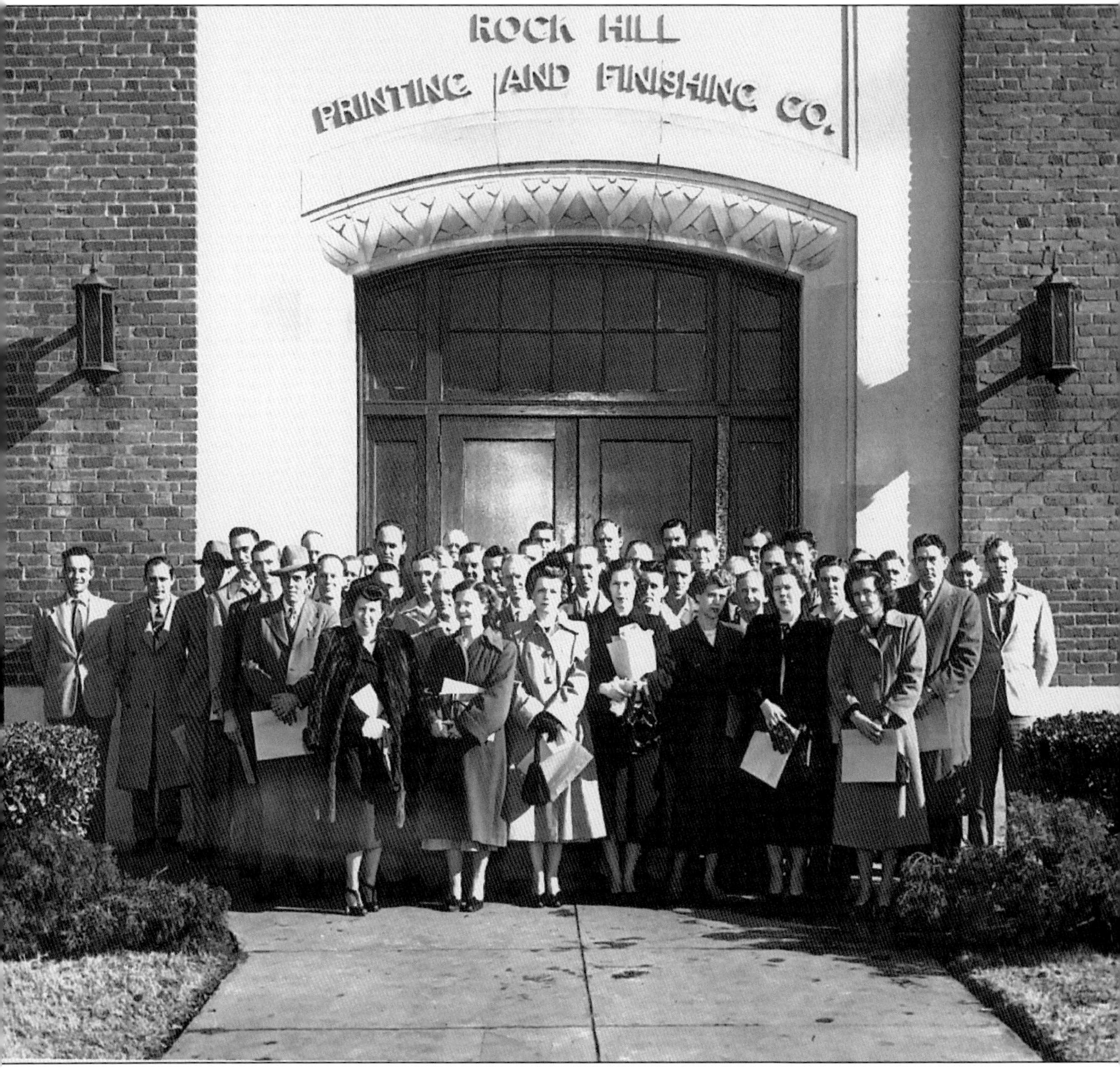

Rock Hill Printing and Finishing Company is shown here in 1950.

remember the Friedham House, and my husband was sort of a carpenter. So, we rebuilt it out at the country club. And we had four children. And it's been a lovely place to live."

"My name is Mary Beth Wick. I came to work at Winthrop Library in 1954 because my parents were living in Charlotte, and they wanted me to be near them.

"So during my time there, they quit wearing the uniforms, and the new library was built, the present library. Mrs. D.B. Johnson was working in the library, and I got to know her real well. And when my mother passed away in Charlotte, my father came down to Rock Hill to live with me. And because he was a minister, Mrs. D.B. Johnson invited us both down for Christmas dinner at her house, and so I knew her real well."

"My name is Esther Edwards. And I know you're going to turn to your neighbor

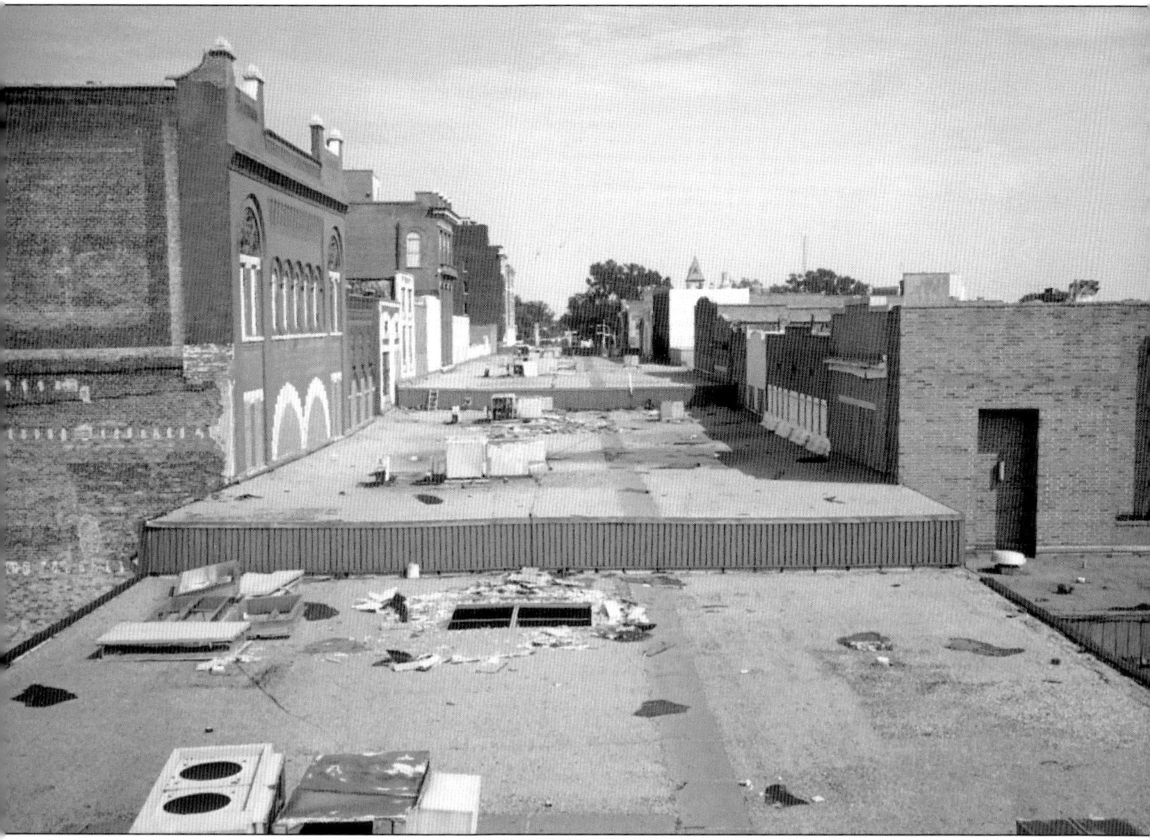

and say, 'Her name isn't that.' I go by 'Peggy.' Allen decided to change my first name before he changed my second. I'm a little surprised that there's been only one notice given concerning the girls' uniforms. I don't think the girls especially liked them, but it was a requirement to wear them. And they looked forward to a Friday afternoon when they would get out of the uniform and put on an ordinary dress, just so it wasn't navy blue and white. And I'm not going to get started on being a faculty wife!

"You could go to Friedham's and buy everything you wanted. Everyone from four or five counties from around here to Friedham's came from Blacksburg and Chester.

"And my husband's family were all into cotton and textiles. It's just coming back now. There's a lot of cotton being planted in York County. I can see it as I drive through. But for all these years in between, I lived 5 miles below, and I could see Rock Hill, and there wasn't a tree between me and the bank building."

"I'm Coreen Rice Handy, and my family had a grocery store and a moving and hauling business. And at that time, you could call in your order if you had a telephone, or someone would come by and knock on your door early in the morning, and if you needed potatoes or whatever for the day and deliver it later on in the afternoon, and that was what my father did. At that time, it was all right to go out and kill an animal, do any kind of butchering you wanted to do, take it in the grocery store, and sell it. I don't know what the health department would say about that, but you could do it then. He'd do all those kinds of things, and then they would meet the train and get all this material that had been shipped in and take it around to different outlying

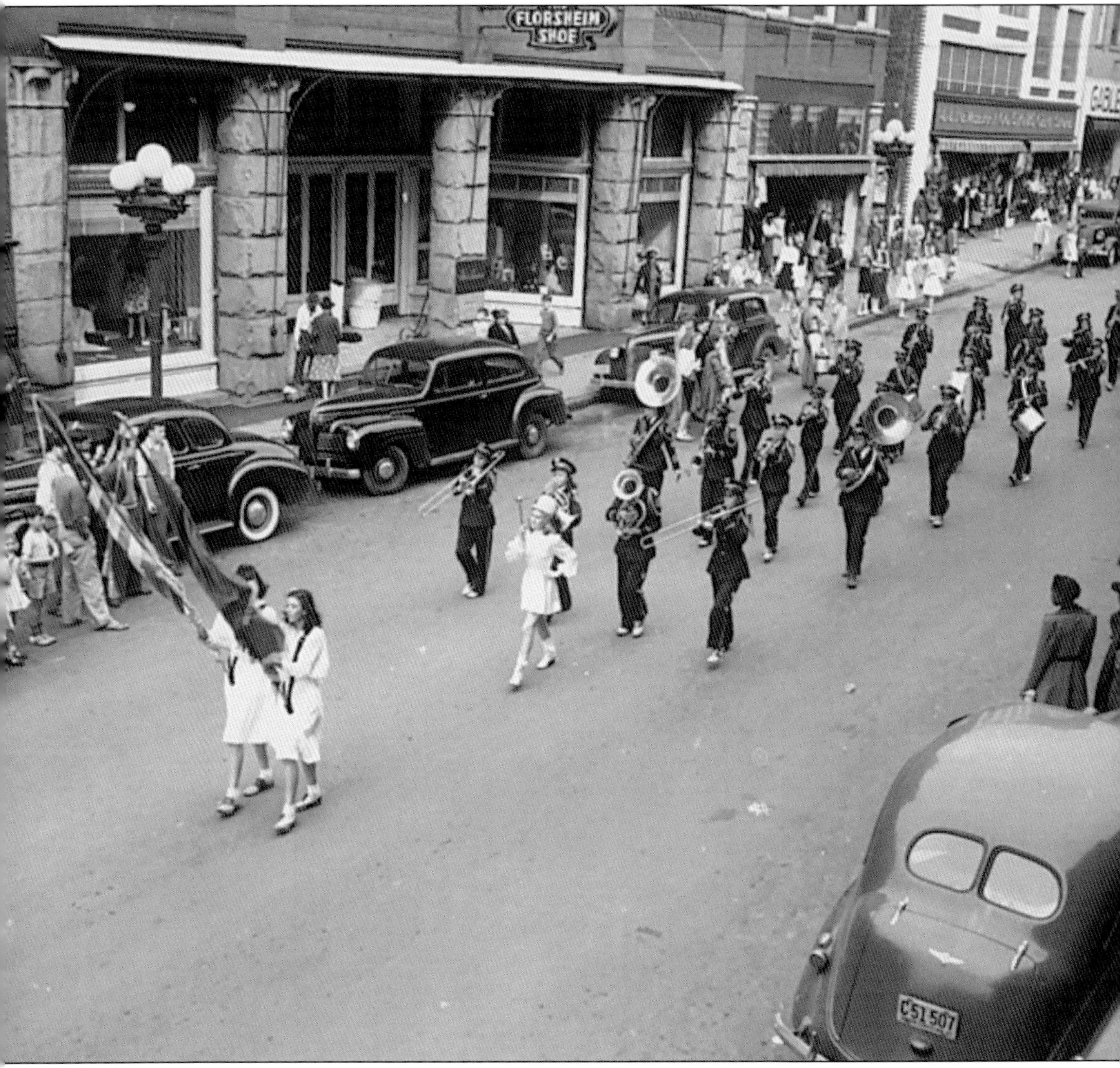

areas out toward Leslie and Lancaster. It was kind of a central place that they would deliver those groceries to. And I remember that in early childhood, my grandfather used to come get us to go to his place out in the country. Every Saturday morning, we'd ride in either a wagon or a buggy and spend half a day behind Friedham's, while he shopped and visited with his cronies, and we'd get so anxious. But that was the way we spent our Saturday mornings, and it was fun."

Dr. Edwards added, "The first mills were started in 1880. There were a number of small mills. When we moved here the Victoria Mills, they did everything. There were Highland Park Mills, and J.P. Stevens Co. had a couple of mills, Aragon and Industrial, and there was another one on Hagins Street. I've forgotten the name of it now, a small mill. Then, around 1929, the printing and finishing company came here. And that was a big thing for Rock Hill because it was just at the beginning of the Depression, and so there was no Depression in Rock Hill compared to other places, because they had this employment there, and I

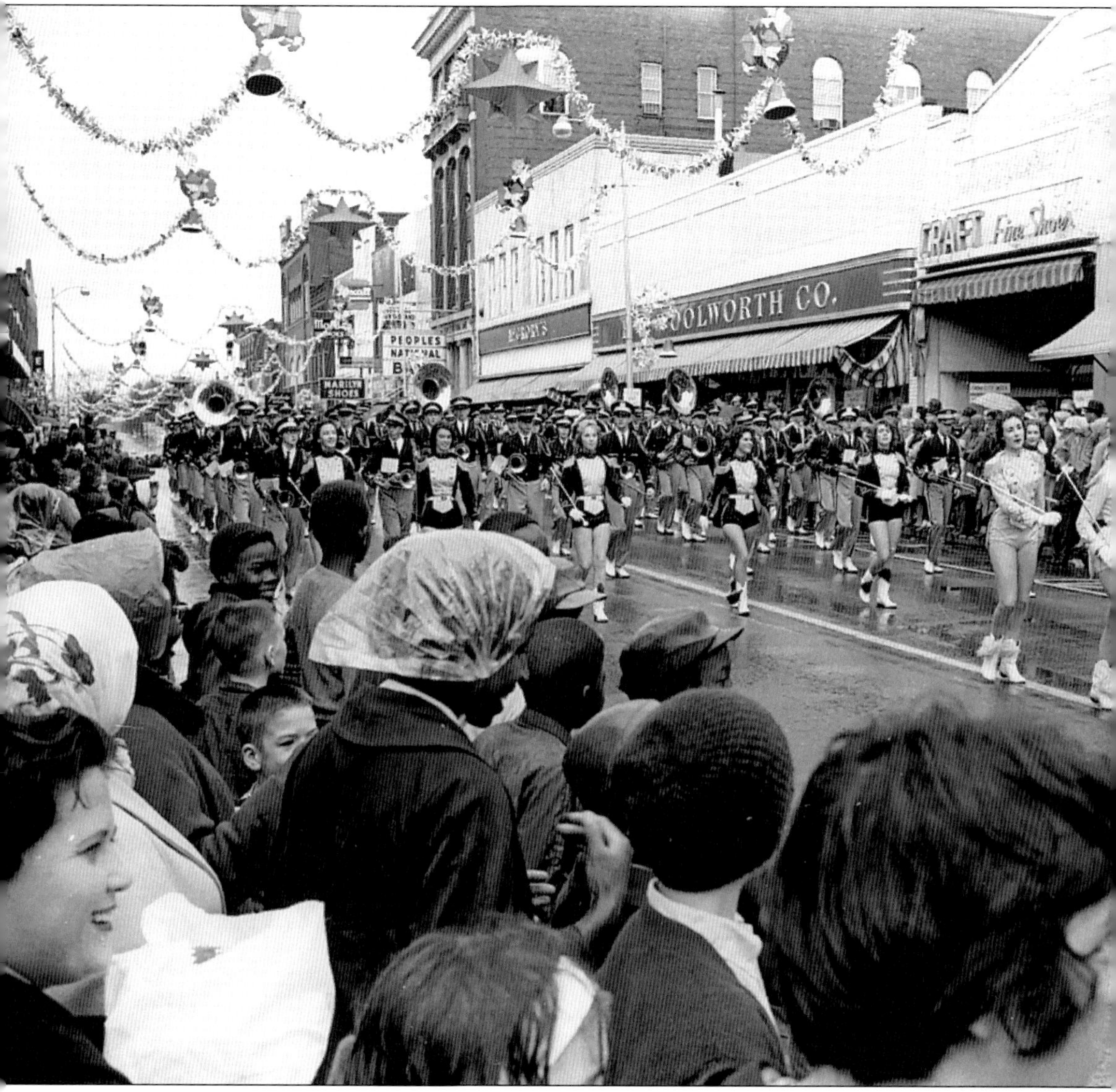

know a lot of people did get employment there. Then, around 1949, Celanese came in and built Rock Hill Homes so that people would have a place to live. Then Bowater came in later. But it's changed now, so much. I know a lot of the international companies. Tech Park I think is remarkable! It's so beautiful. They have international offices out there.

"It wasn't until about 1960 that there were any black students in Winthrop. The mills, in the beginning, had their own villages, so that separated them out, and socially, they became separate, schools and stores and churches. Now when the Rock Hill Printing and Finishing came here, they didn't build any houses. So the employees of Rock Hill were not separated. They were not considered mill workers, although they did the same kind of work, essentially."

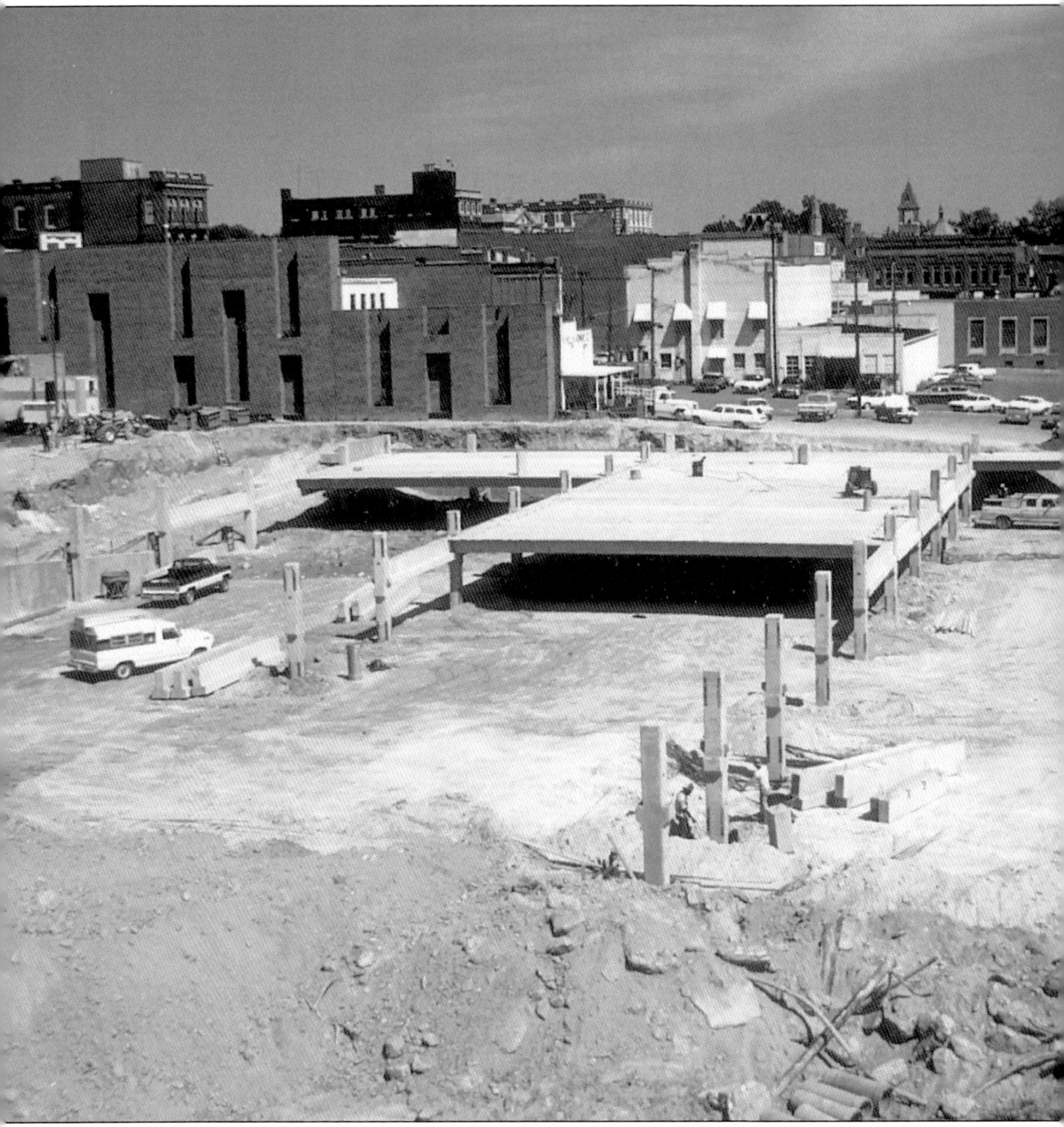

CHEERLEADER

Betty Jo Dunlap Rhea has always energetically championed the causes of her hometown, whether they were sons (and husbands) risking their lives on far away battlefields, or the need for neighborhood parks, or gender equality, or the shift to a diverse economy, or an activist municipal government. After two decades in elective office, Mrs. Rhea retired in 1998 as mayor of Rock Hill, but she still remains a tireless cheerleader for the gateway to the New South.

"I was born right here in Rock Hill. My father was a doctor here. He was born here as well. My mother was from Philadelphia. He met here when he went to Penn Medical School. My father's parents were born here as

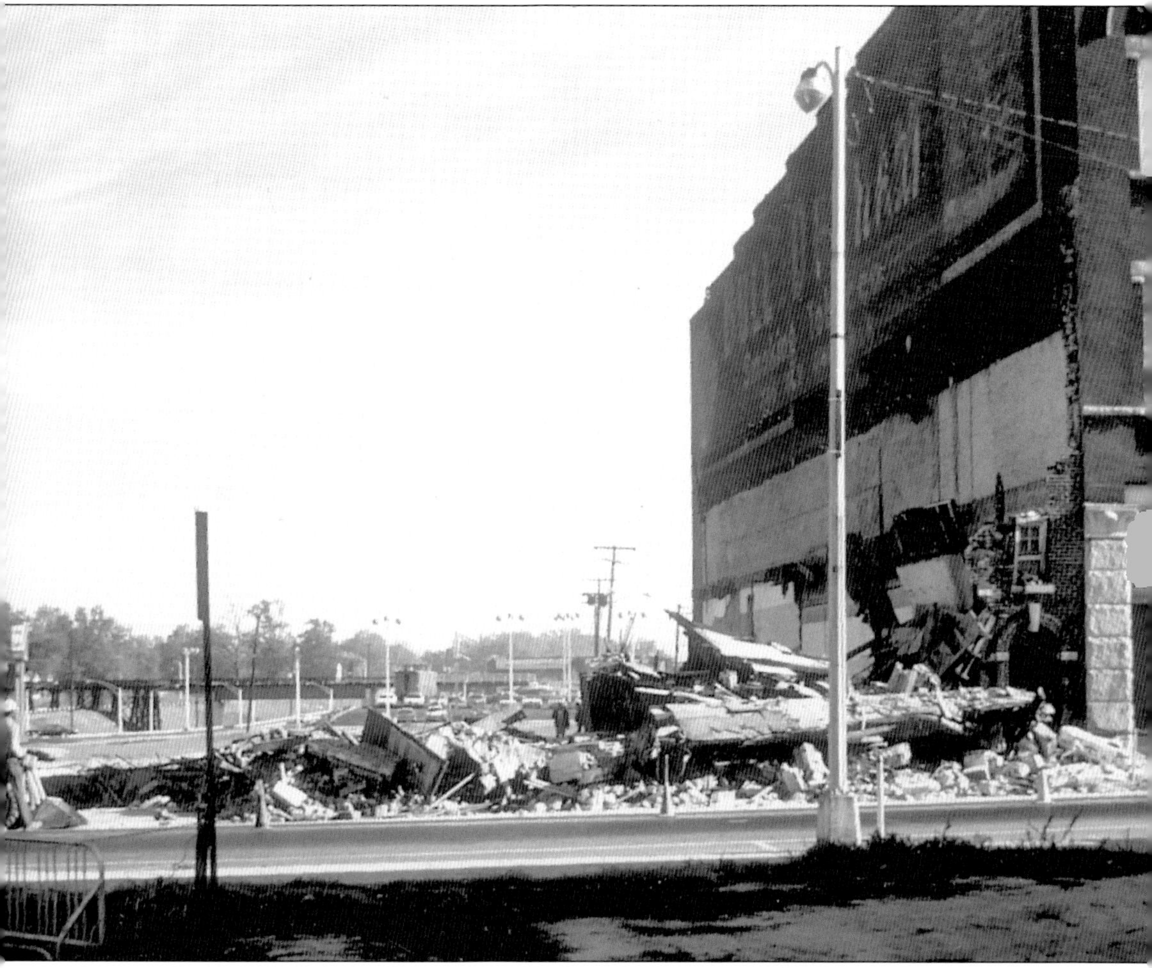

well. My grandmother on my dad's side was from York. She was a Dunlap, married a Dunlap. I've lived in Rock Hill all my life.

"I went to Barry College in Miami, Florida, and then I came back and went to Winthrop. And then I got married. I went back to Winthrop after my children were born.

"This is how I got involved in politics. One summer, when I was in the Junior League, we needed someone to teach swimming to these little underprivileged girls. We had a Worthy Girls Camp. And so, I volunteered to teach swimming that summer. I got real involved with that program. We asked the head of the parks and recreation department to come out at the end of our camp and give all the little girls a blue ribbon. He went to my church. He asked if I would be interested in serving on the parks and recreation commission. I said, 'I think I would like that.' So, I served on that commission for nine years and chaired it for three years. I was on the parks and recreation commission when we did all the neighborhood parks.

"When I chaired the commission, I started going to the city council meetings to let the mayor and council know that I appreciated what they were doing for recreation. And there was a council election coming up. There would be two seats up, and I decided to run. It was 'at large' then. We didn't have districts. As a matter of fact, I have always run 'at large.' When I ran for the city council in 1978, I think there were

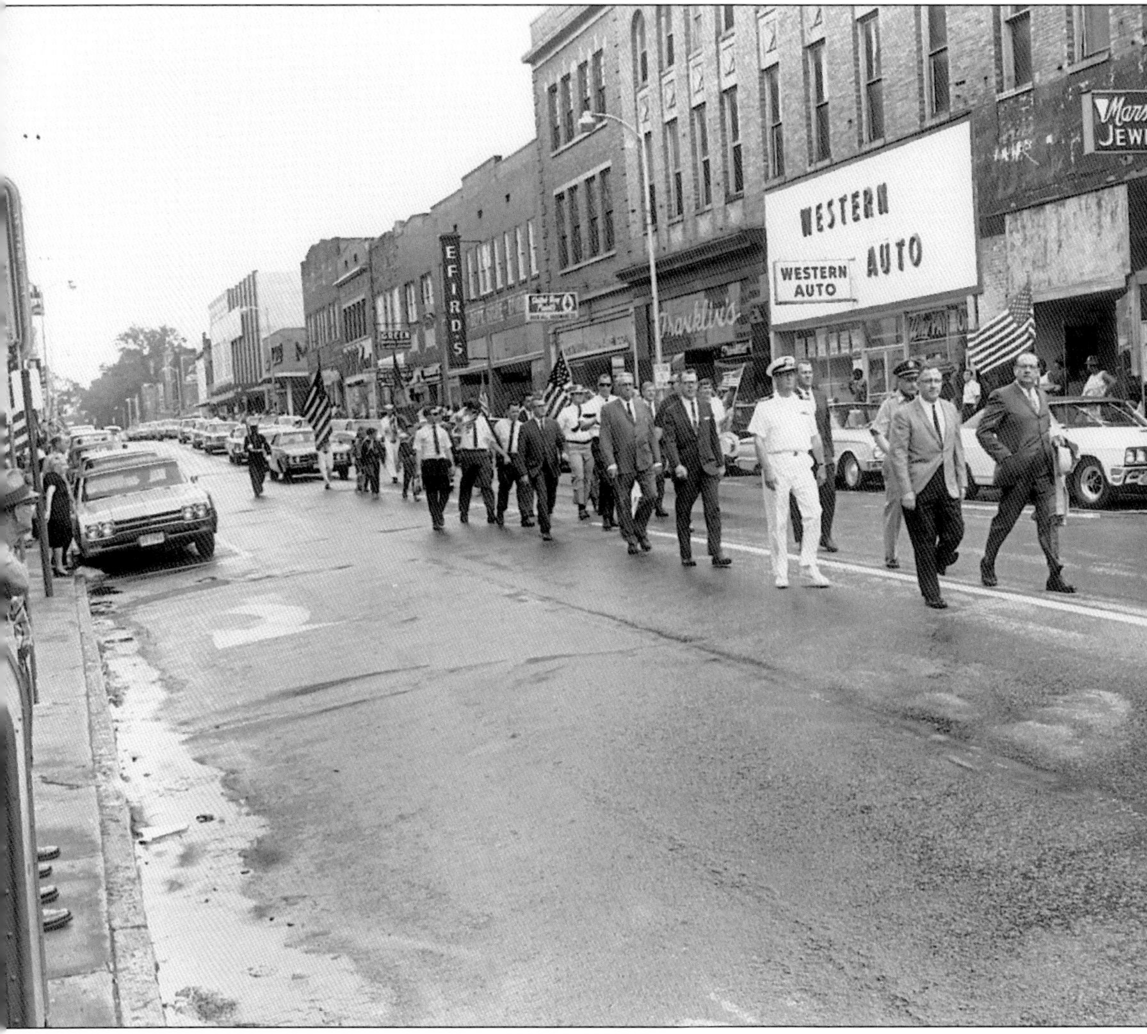

nine people running. I won on the first ballot, which was real unusual. I served on the council for eight years.

"I wasn't going to run again, but there wasn't anyone out there who had the same ideas I had, so I decided to run for mayor. When I first got elected, I didn't feel a real bias against women. You know, a lot of people knew me, knew what I had done. I had been active in the community all my life. My husband, Jimmy, had been active, too. I did find that a lot of my friends' husbands didn't vote for me because I was a woman. There was *that feeling out there.* I found it on the state level and on the national level. It's still there. One time, I was the only woman on the U. S. Conference of Mayors Board of Trustees. I served on the nominating committee several times, and it was hard to get women in there.

"I think a lot of my success nationally was because I was a Southern woman. People really liked the Southern accent and the gentleness of a Southern woman. It was probably one of my biggest assets.

"As a child, I can remember walking down Main Street in Rock Hill. You know, there were businesses downstairs. And there were these grates, and you could look down through the grates. I was always afraid that I might fall through!

"My daddy's office was where the Baptist Church's office building is on Caldwell

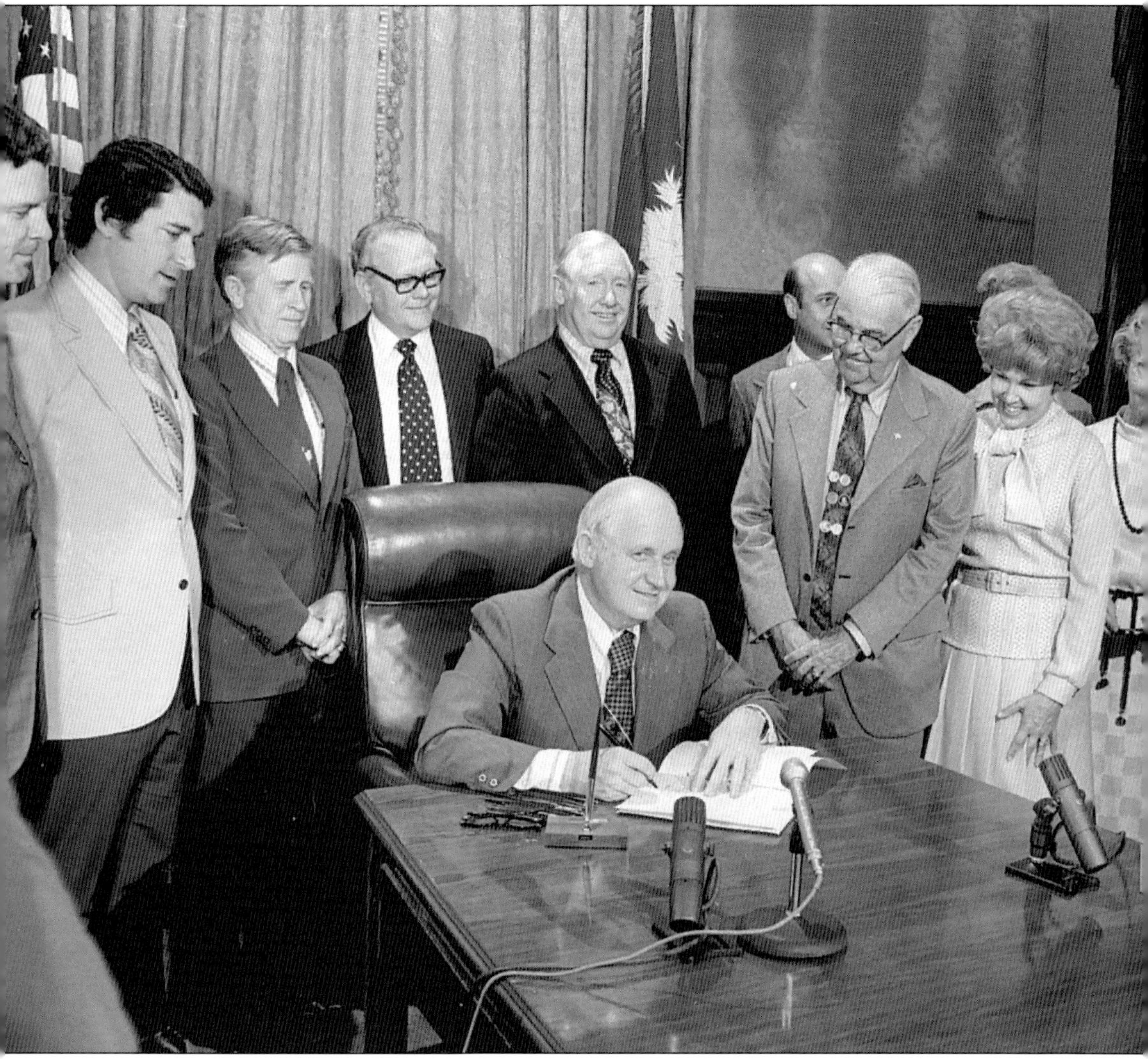

Governor West signed Winthrop's coeducation legislature in 1974.

Street. I remember when they were building his office, they moved the houses on the lot to St. John's Court. The building that used to be the library was on Main Street, and they moved it.

"My daddy came back after med school and lived on Pendleton Street. He practiced with Dr. Ward. His office was upstairs over Phillips Drug Store on Main Street. I was born at Fennell Infirmary.

"I remember when they had the maneuvers here. We lived where the Harris Teeter is on Cherry Road, and the convoys would come by. Cherry Road was a two lane road then. The convoys would be parked there at night, and we would have our lights turned off.

"My mother and father were both pilots, and during the Second World War, they became active in the Civil Air Patrol. And they flew on weekends along the South Carolina coast. My father wrote my mother after a flight: 'you would be shocked if I told you what I have seen today.' In 1943, when the military cadets were training at Winthrop, my mother taught meteorology and first aid to the cadets.

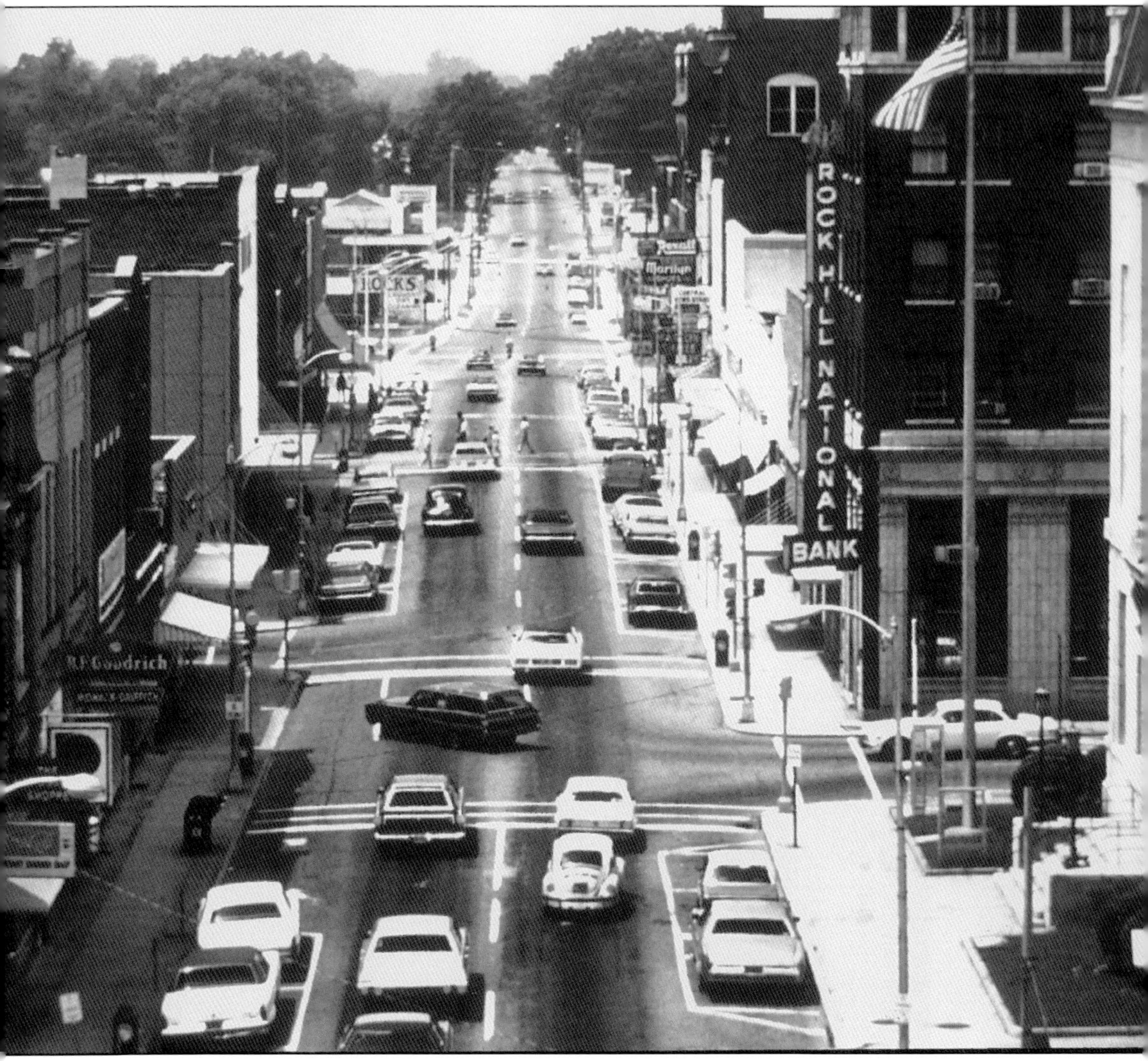

This early 1970s photograph shows the downtown business district.

"All my father's sisters went to Winthrop. I remember, as a little girl, the wonderful artists' series they had on campus. We had opera stars, performers of all kinds, a fantastic music program! Ann Herlong's mother, a senior at Winthrop, performed once when an orchestra's pianist couldn't perform. At the end, the philharmonic stood up and gave her a standing ovation.

"When they had the sit-ins at the dime stores and at Good's Drug Store, I remember all the press people being here. Jimmy was on the national news. He was in Good's Drug Store drinking a Coke when they came in. People got involved to keep us from having the kinds of problems other communities experienced. People like Brother David Boone, Bill Barron, Reverend Toatley, Wade Witherspoon stopped those kinds of things.

"The fact is that we have looked at ourselves as a historic city. The columns on Dave Lyle Boulevard are supposed to be replicas of the ones on King Solomon's Tomb. We had them

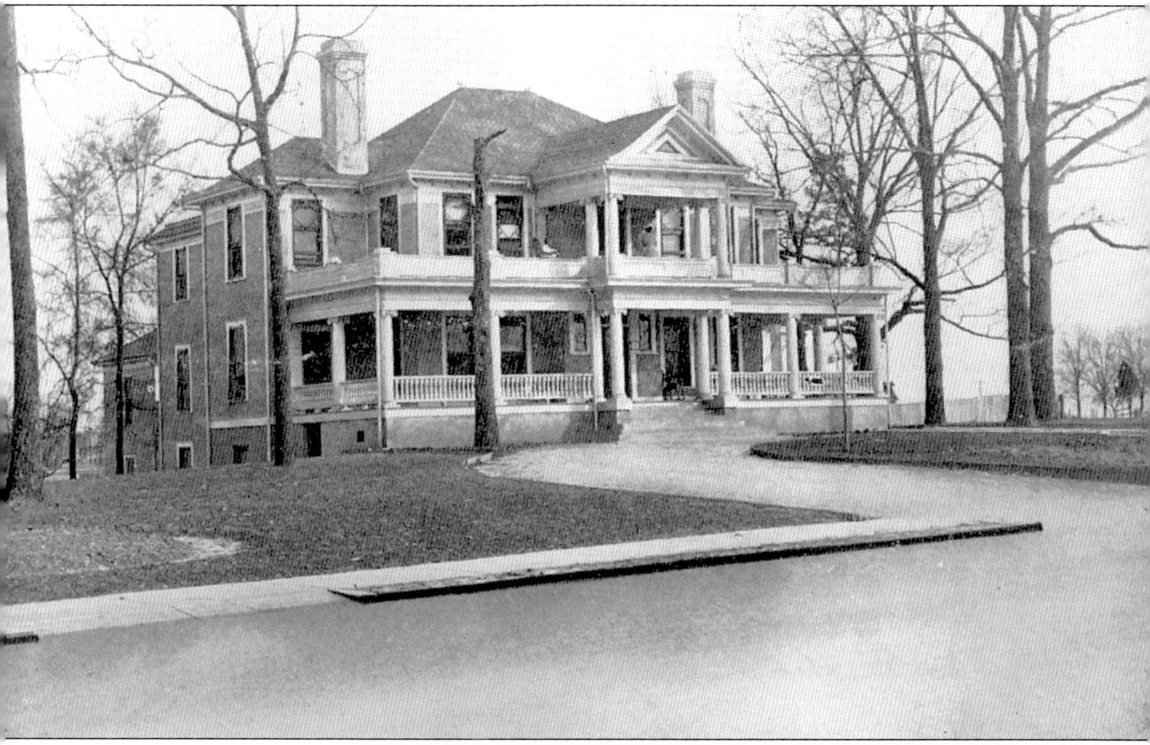

Fennell Hospital is pictured here.

appraised when we first got them at $700,000. They've been done over now and are worth much, much more. Each sculpture stands for something. The one with the stars stands for a cultural city. The one with the flame stands for an educational city. The one that has the gears represents the business city. The one that has the water and lightening is a functional city. So, those are the ways we looked at ourselves during our Empowering the Vision effort. And the circle represents us all working together. And the plantings represent the garden city. The columns represent the historic city. Each one represents how we see ourselves. The sculpture is on her toes, which symbolizes a forward looking city.

"We have tried to save our history. When we took the roof off Main Street, we could see all those buildings we had preserved. We try to do things better than they have to be, and the city hall speaks well for that goal.

"Cherry Park is one of my greatest successes. The quality of life issues, and the environmental issues were addressed. It was just a field. The other thing is re-economizing our city. When I became mayor, we were at 17.29% unemployment, and we worked together as a team. We had vision. We had 13 textile mills. They all closed but one. We worked together to get the city where it is today. That is remarkable! I always felt I was the cheerleader. A lot of other people had good ideas, but I could cheer along the side."

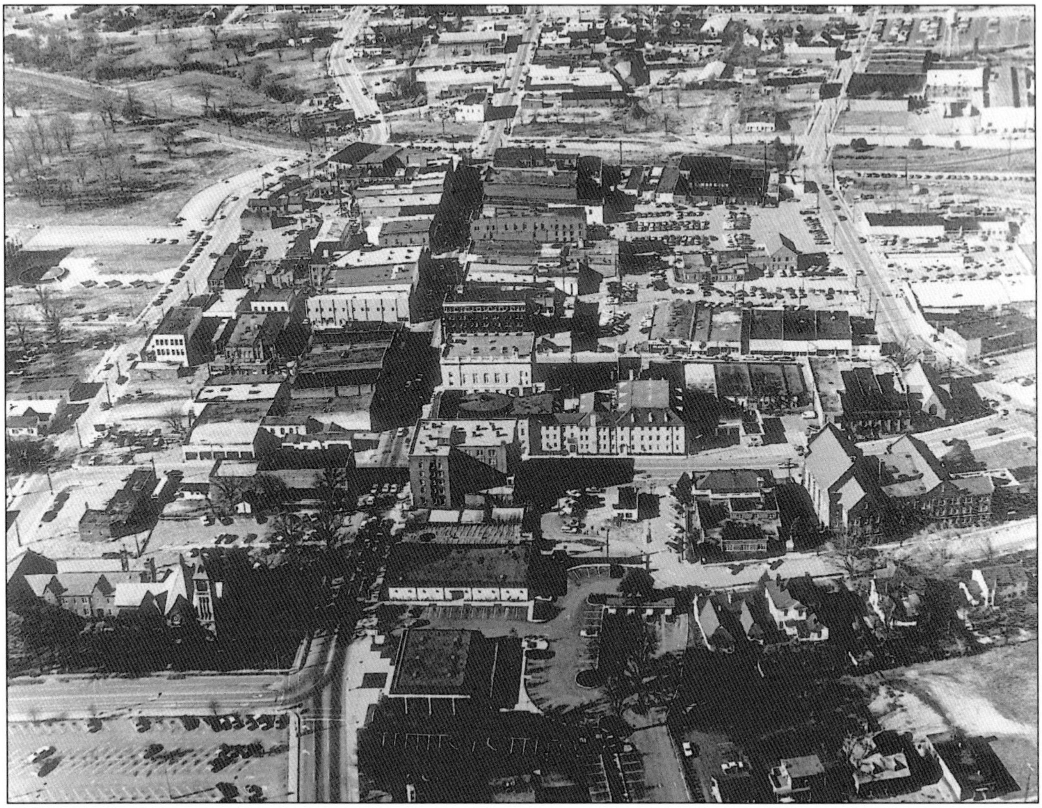

AGRONOMIST BANKER

From the time he graduated from Clemson College until he retired after 33 years as a Rock Hill banker, the late Jack Hutcheson was a prominent figure in the business community. Prior to his demise, Mr. Hutcheson shared with us his reflections about changes in this New South city.

"I came to Rock Hill in 1936. At that time, I was engaged to get married to a girl in Newberry. Her father was a Lutheran minister. He taught at Newberry College, and I had already been to him and asked him about it and everything, and everything was fine. So I moved on up here, stayed here a few months, and this girl and I were writing each other every day. She'd write me, and I'd write her every day, and

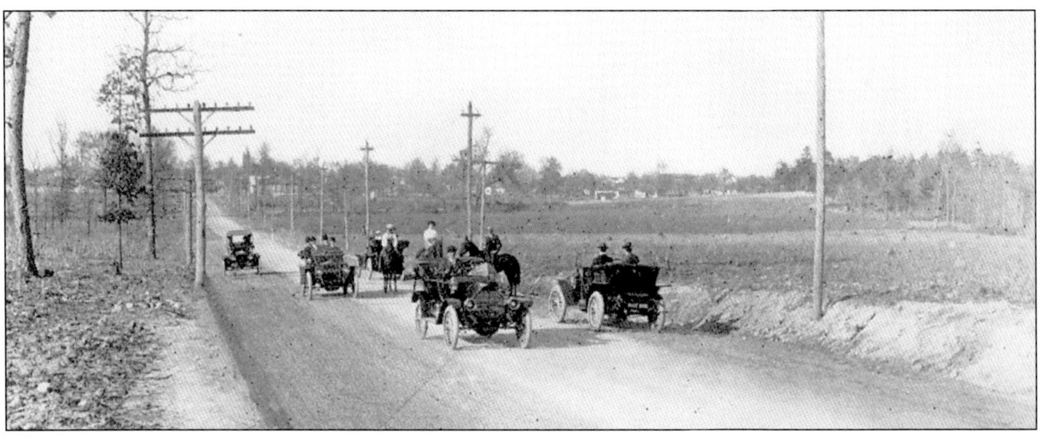

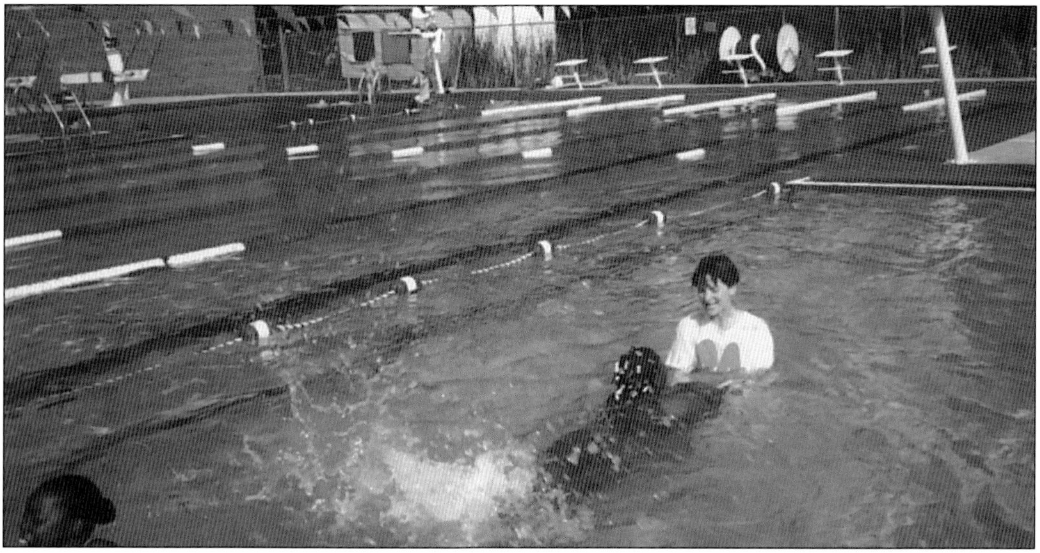

Pools and parks are integral parts of this New South City.

all of a sudden, I looked up on the mantle, and there were about six or eight letters from her that I hadn't opened. And I said well now something's gone wrong here. By that time, I had started going with Lill Dunlap, the wife who died in 1967. So, the Sunday afternoon after that, I drove down to North, South Carolina, where this girl from Newberry was teaching. We decided the best thing to do was to call it off, and we did.

"You asked about the Marshall House. Well you see what happened was, Lill and I moved into the Dunlap House, next door.

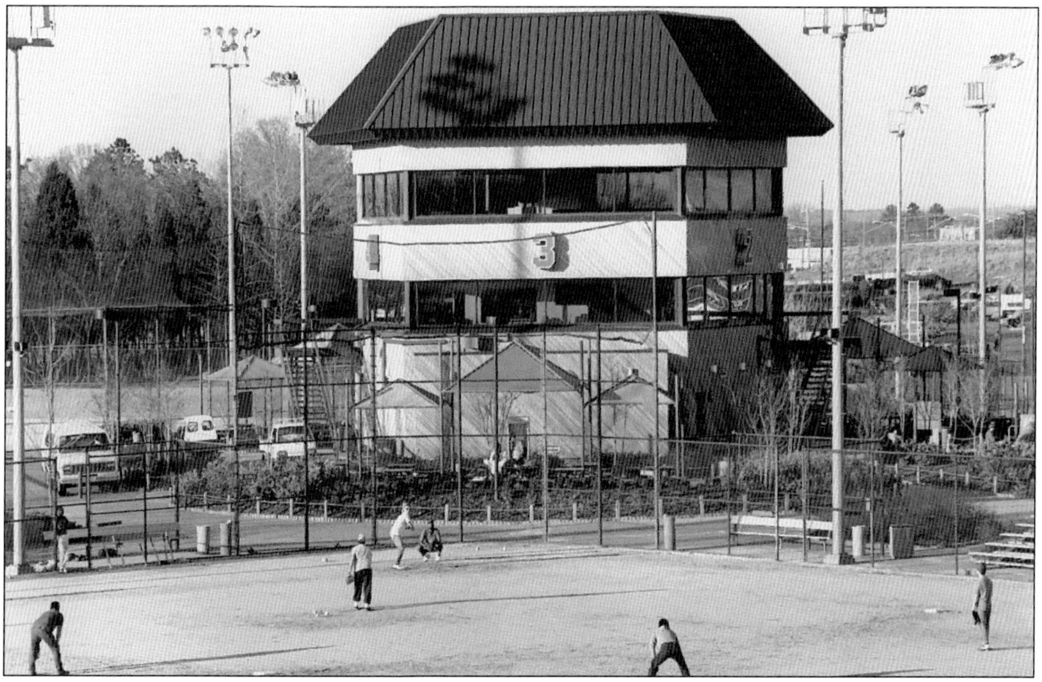

Cherry Park is pictured here.

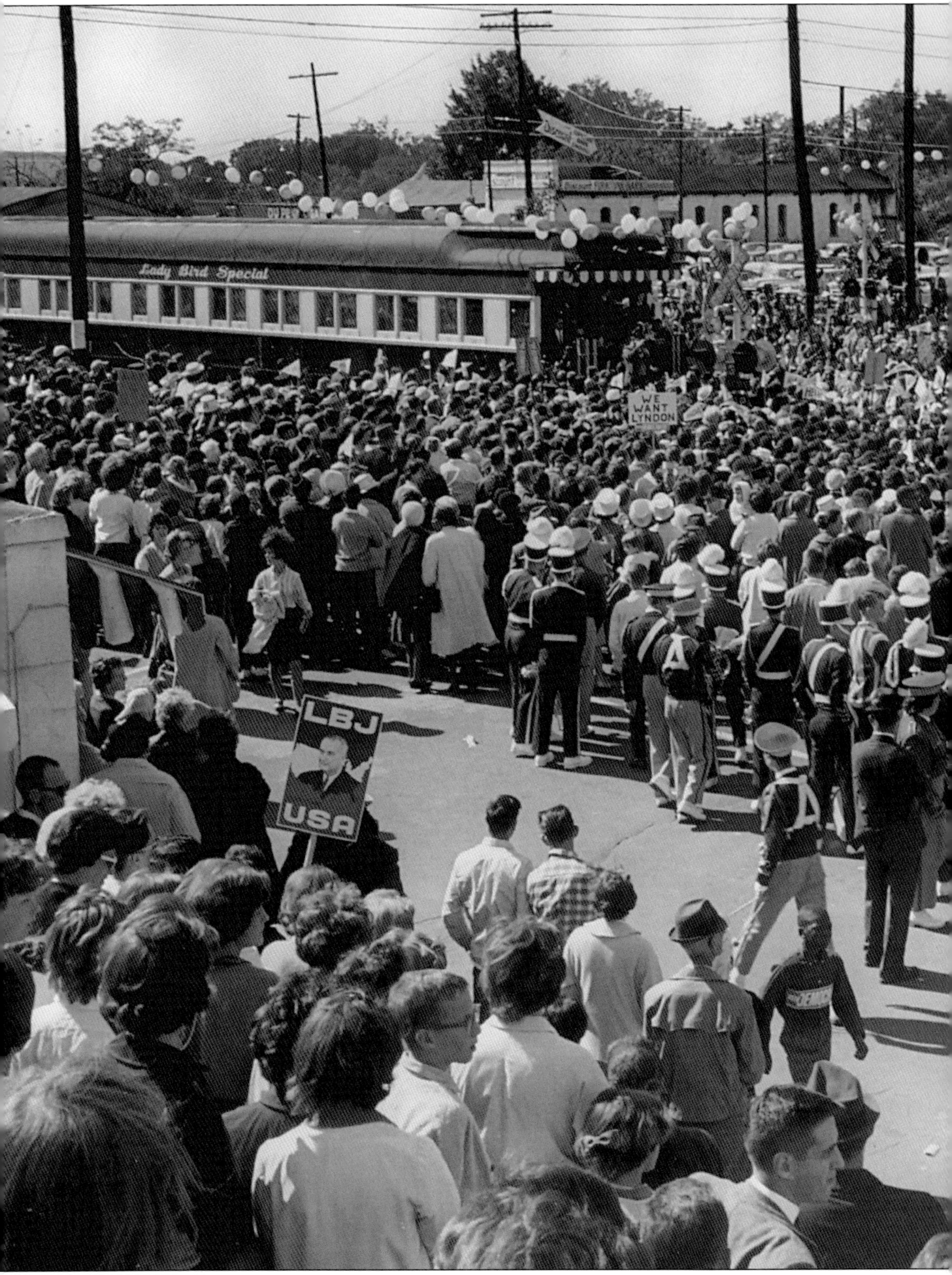

Lady Bird Johnson campaigns for her husband, President Lyndon Johnson, in the

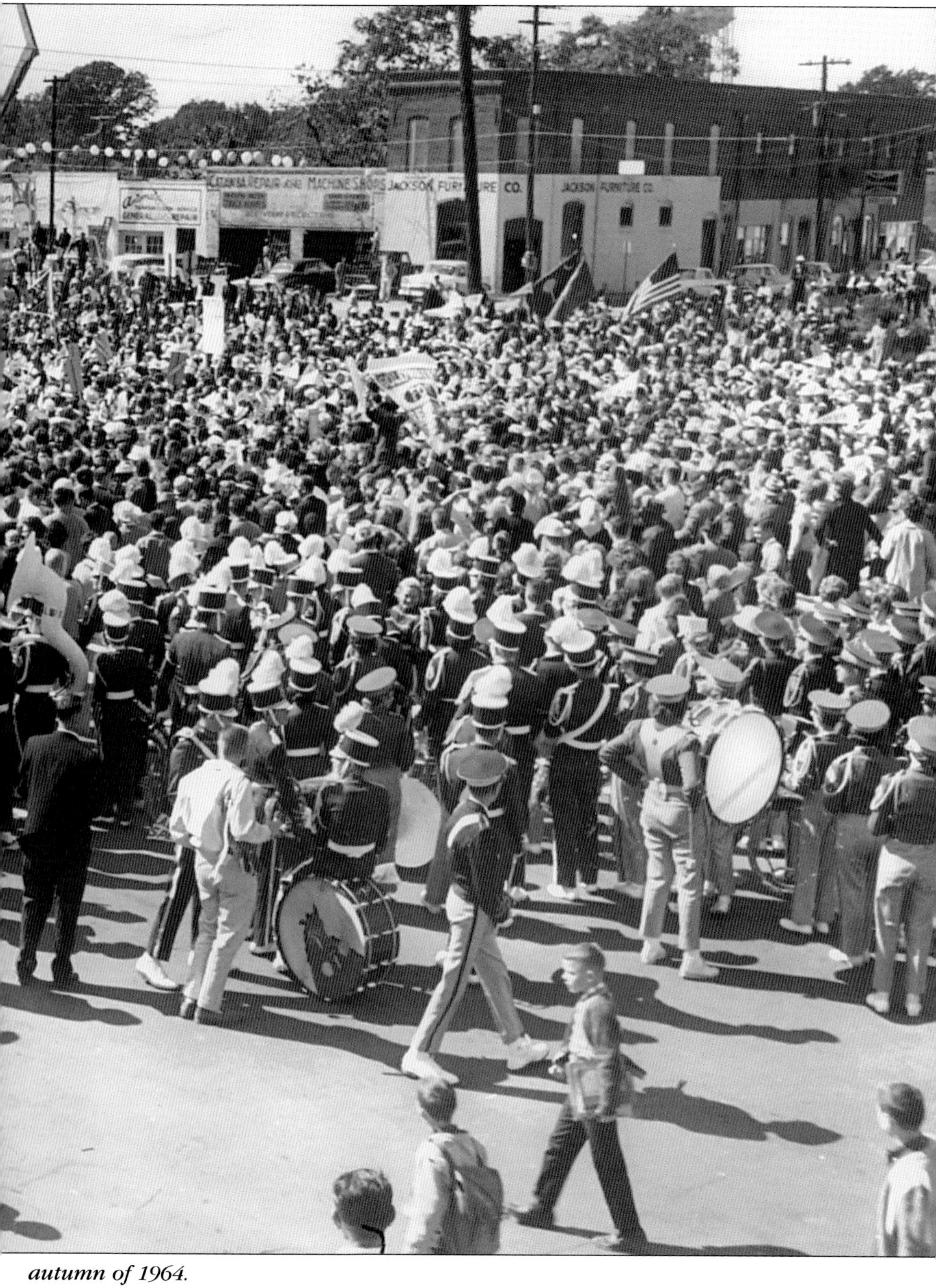

autumn of 1964.

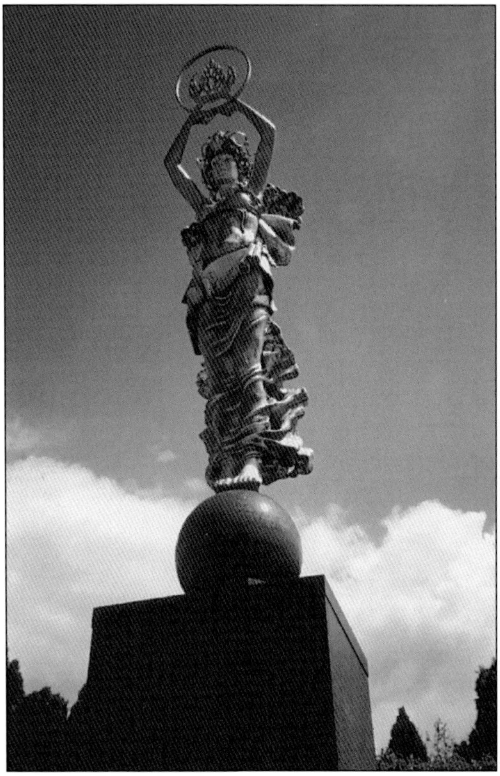

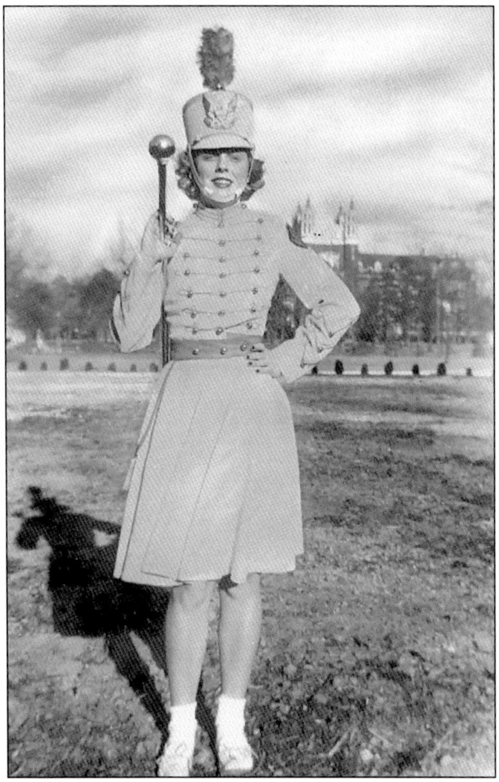

We moved there in 1945, I guess it was, or '46 because that's when I came back from the service, and her older sister was staying there with their mother. Their father had been badly injured in the service, and they had to leave and go be with him. So Lill and I came back there to live. I was working in Hartsville at the time at Coker Seed Company, so I gave up that job and came back to Rock Hill in 1946, I guess it was, and we lived there until, well, I lived there until 1969. I lived there two years after she died. She died in 1967, and all three of our children were raised in that house. We were not living there when they were born, but they were all three raised in that house. They all three went all the way through high school and didn't have to be more than a block and a half from home from grammar school through Central School and Rock Hill High School.

"We lived there until 1969 and then after Lill died. Jean had moved back to Rock Hill and was living with her mother, Mrs. Twitty, and she didn't have room for a studio that she wanted. The Marshall House was just sitting there vacant and deteriorating, so she bought it. Then we got to seeing each other, and I've always accused her of kicking the back fence down between the two houses. Anyway, we got married in 1969. I stayed single for two years. Then we lived in the Marshall House from 1969 until 1990, when we moved up here.

"Looking back, after the war and the changes in Rock Hill, you didn't have too many because there was nothing to change with. Everything was being used for the war effort. There were streetcar rails that had been dug up and made into bullets. The rails came down a Main Street and ran all around downtown. I don't know whether that happened while I was gone or not, but it did happen.

"Business began to change real rapidly after the war. Not too many changes between the time I left and when I came back. Lill and the two girls lived down on

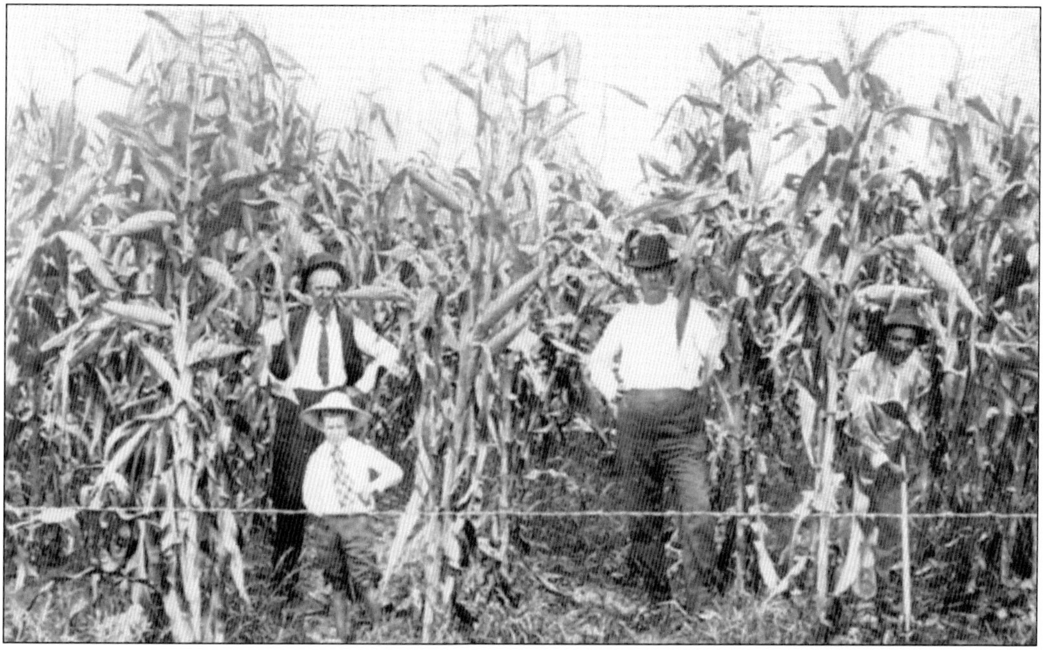

Milton Avenue during the war. I recall the first time I came home. I was coming home from Memphis, Tennessee, on the train, and the train ahead of us had a wreck at Seneca, South Carolina. They said it was going to be half a day, maybe, or a day getting cleared up, so we could come on home. I got off the train and walked to town, which was about a mile, and found a cab driver and asked him how much he'd charge me to bring me to Rock Hill. He said $37, and I said, 'Crank it up.' We got here way up in the night. I didn't know where 706 Milton was, so I made him take me to the Rock Hill taxi stand, and I paid him off and let him go and let the Rock Hill taxi take me to Milton Avenue.

"My business in Rock Hill—I was in the bank for 33 years. I was also in the insurance business for a few years, but I came here with the U.S. Department of Agriculture, Soil and Conservation Science. By the grace of God and Clemson College, I have a degree in agronomy, so I could spend my life in a bank.

"After the war, the city of Rock Hill got grants, and they built some things. They put up several buildings. They found out after they got them built, I think, that there were unauthorized. They built that stone building over there close to the stadium. That was being used, when I got back here, by the American Legion. Anyway, they found out that it was not an authorized reason for building. And the country club, the WPA built that, too. Originally they did. Incidentally, I was the first president of the Rock Hill Country Club when it was bought from the city of Rock Hill, and I don't even play golf. I was also the first World War II Commander of the American Legion here.

"People who came back from World War II were treated so different than veterans from the Korean and the Vietnamese Wars, because people appreciated what had been done. And these other two, they were just kind of, it was terrible the way those people had been treated.

"There've been some major changes in the city since I came here in 1936. I think closing in downtown was the stupidest thing I have ever seen. Businesses didn't survive. They all eventually closed up. I don't know whether they'll get it to come back now or not. The Friedham building is a beautiful building, but I don't know yet how much it'll draw.

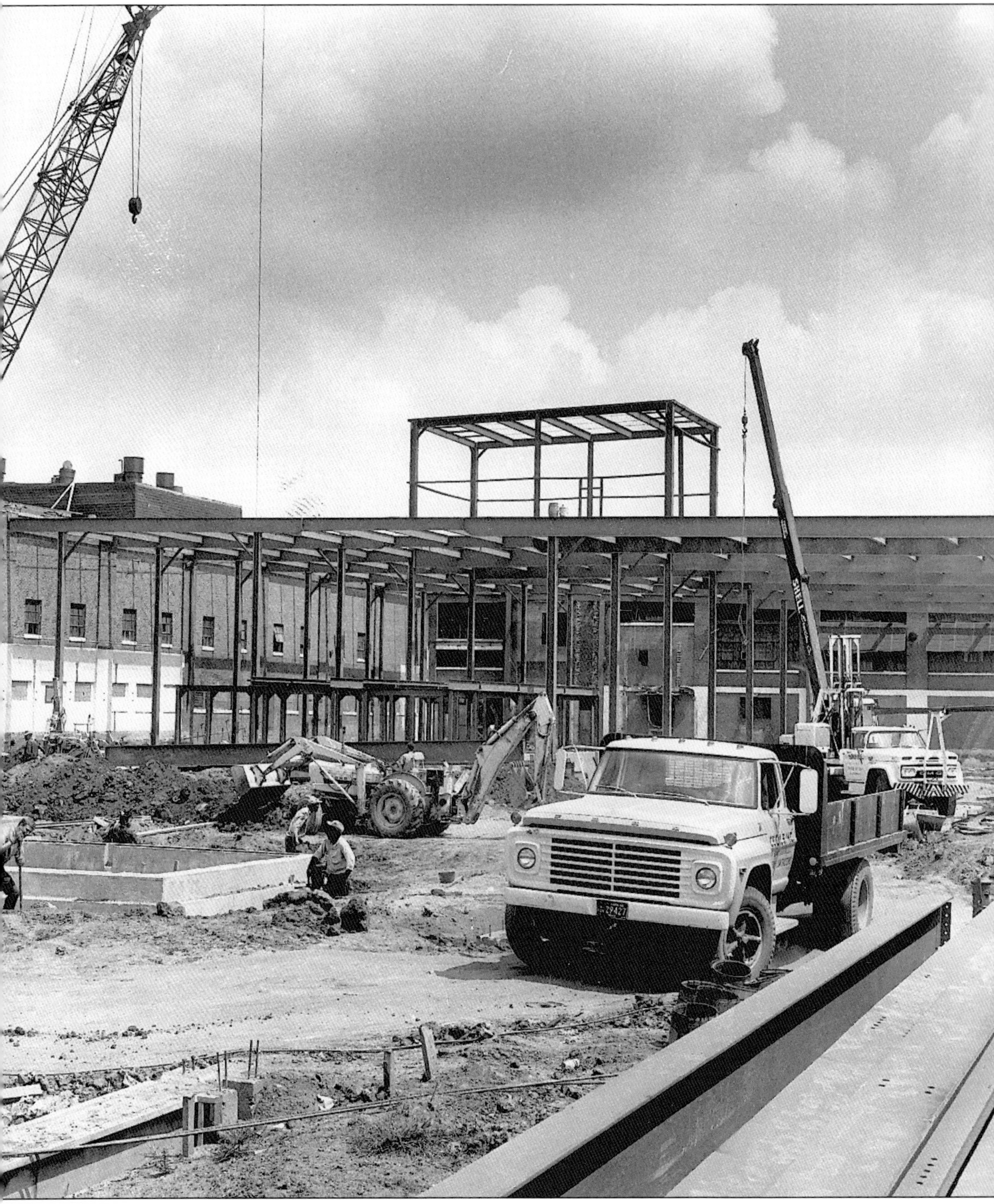

"The city has moved out to the parameters, out to the shopping centers, as far as business is concerned. Earlier you could go from five or six blocks away and be at the middle of the business section. Now, you got to drive 2 or 3 miles to get there. Right now, to go to the Galleria, it is a 14-mile roundtrip for us here (at Westminister Towers). One of the fastest growing sections around here is on the corner of Herlong and Heckle. That place is really thriving, really growing.

"When we look at the growth in Rock

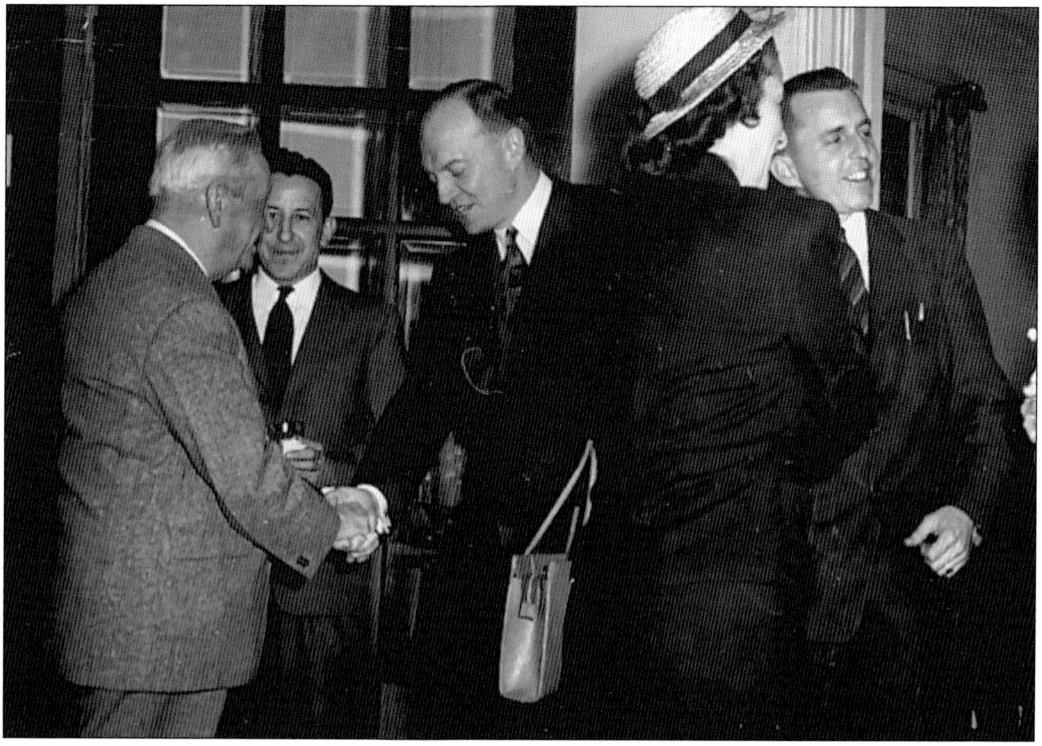

In 1946, a group of business leaders welcomed Minnesota's ex-governor, Harold Stassen, to Rock Hill.

Hill, the Bleachery, at the time, was the biggest thing that ever happened here. That was in 1929. I wasn't living here at the time, but I heard about it. And it gave hundreds and hundreds of people jobs that hadn't had a job for a long time. They, at one time, worked/employed 5,000 people. I don't know what they got over there now, probably 12 to 1,400. See, we used to have 14 textile plants in Rock Hill. We don't have any of that now unless you count the Bleachery. Bowater was a big financial

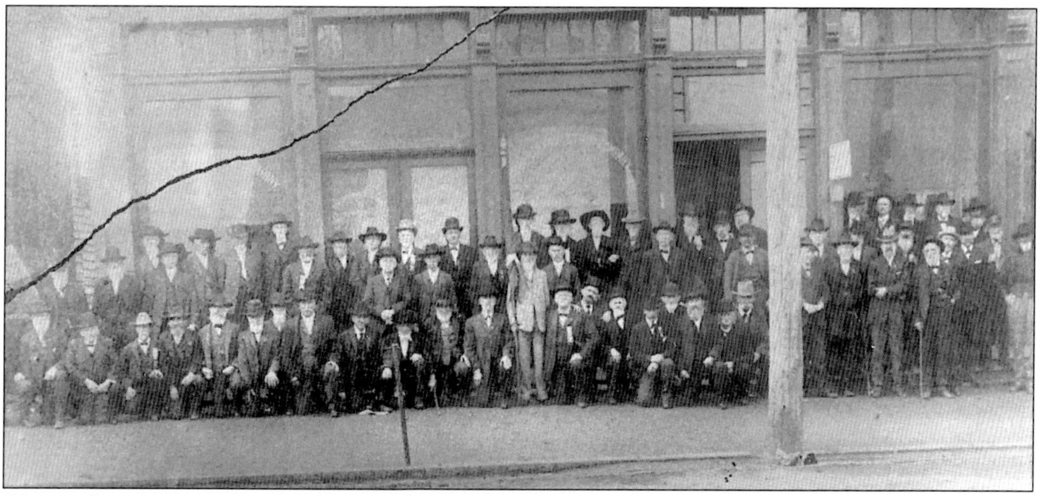

Shown here is a reunion of Confederate veterans in 1931.

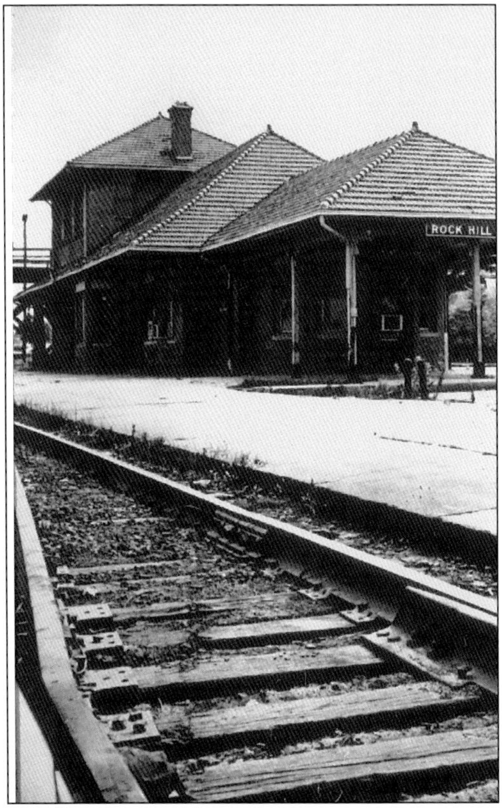

boost to Rock Hill and others, Celanese. There are so many little businesses in and around Rock Hill, in these commercial areas, and if you add all those together and give credit for the diversity that it furnishes, you may have a better deal there than you'd have in one big outfit, because they wouldn't all close at one time.

"Charlotte's always had a terrible impact on Rock Hill as far as drawing Rock Hill dollars away. Twenty years ago, I knew people that would live here and go to Charlotte and buy their groceries and go there and buy their clothes, and lots of them still do, of course. Charlotte is a big, big drain on Rock Hill retail business and always has been and probably always will be, until the two towns grow together, which they are going to do. I don't know whether that's good or bad, but it is going to happen one of these days."

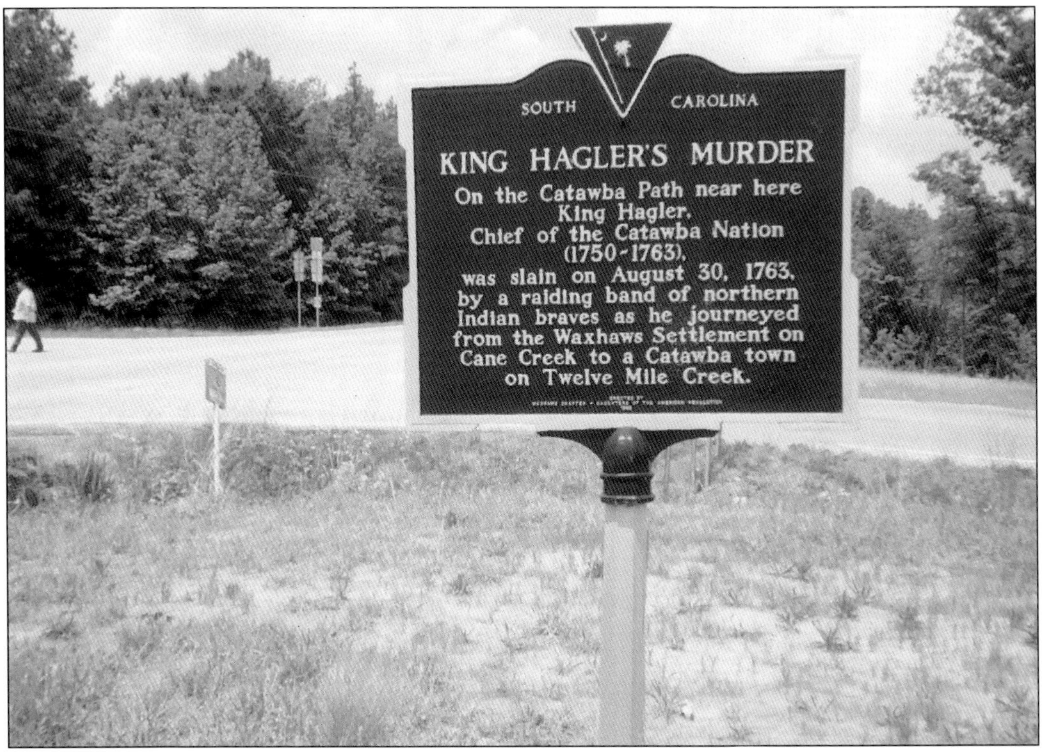